TO THE
MAX

TO THE
MAX

Revenue Maximization:
Capturing The Opportunities Within
by
Randy Browning and
Sameer Kumar

TO THE MAX—Revenue Maximization: Capturing The Opportunities Within
Copyright © 2003 PricewaterhouseCoopers.

PricewaterhouseCoopers refers to the network of member firms of
PricewaterhouseCoopers International Limited, each of which is a
separate and independent legal entity. All rights reserved.

This document is provided by PricewaterhouseCoopers for general guidance only, and does not constitute the provision of legal advice, accounting services, investment advice, or professional consulting of any kind. The information provided herein should not be used as a substitute consultation with professional tax, accounting, legal, or other competent advisers. Before making any decision or taking any action, you should consult a professional adviser who has been provided with all pertinent facts relevant to your particular situation.

The information is provided "as is," with no assurance or guarantee of completeness, accuracy, or timeliness of the information, and without warranty of any kind, express or implied, including but not limited to warranties of performance, merchantability, and fitness for a particular purpose.

No part of this publication may be reproduced, stored in a retrieval system or transmitted in any form or by any means, electronic, mechanical, photocopying, recording, scanning or otherwise, except as permitted under Sections 107 or 108 of the 1976 United States Copyright Act, without either the prior written permission of PricewaterhouseCoopers, or authorization through payment of the appropriate per-copy fee to the Copyright Clearance Center, 222 Rosewood Drive, Danvers, MA 01923. Requests to PricewaterhouseCoopers for permission should be addressed to Office of General Counsel, PricewaterhouseCoopers, 1301 Avenue of the Americas, New York, NY 10019.

Additional books may be purchased for educational or business use. For information, visit our Web site: **www.revenuemaximization.com**

Browning, Randy.
  To the max — revenue maximization : capturing the opportunities within/Randy Browning and Sameer Kumar.
  1. Management — Financial Performance
  2. Communication Industries — Process Improvement I. Kumar, Sameer II. Title
  ISBN 1-931684-06-5

*To my wife Tammy,
my daughters, Jordan and Lindsay
and my parents, Duane and Betty.
—R.B.*

*To my wife Cynthia,
my son, Aydan
and my parents, Bala and Santosh.
—S.K.*

*From both of us, to the ICAS partners
and staff globally.*

Foreword

In the aftermath of the recent highly publicized corporate scandals, integrity and quality have become the watchword among today's top executives. Unlike the exuberant days of the dot-coms, during which astonishing rates of growth and profitability may have caused the markets, media, regulators, and investing public to be less attentive with regard to possible improprieties, the current environment will not tolerate any breaches in corporate integrity. Today, executives know that they have no choice but to ensure that their personal reputations and that of the organizations they represent are unimpeachable. This is as it should be.

It has also become clear that corporate integrity need not be at odds with profitability and growth. But intense scrutiny and a sobering economy have made achieving those critical objectives more difficult than at any time during the past decade. Whereas companies were once able to seize the value created from major restructuring efforts, merger synergies, new technologies, expanding global markets, and unprecedented economic growth; many executives are now wondering how they will be able to deliver the profit growth their shareholders demand while maintaining the integrity required by all stakeholders. The answer for many companies is a return to core operations improvement. As detailed in this book, a revenue maximization strategy, when properly implemented, can provide executives with the tools they need to deliver on all fronts: growth, improved profitability, and—crucially—stronger quality and integrity.

The premise of revenue maximization is a simple one, and the authors of this book state it succinctly: Companies should collect "all the revenue and only the revenue" they deserve. Capturing that deserved revenue can, as the strategy has proven time and again, generate real, sizable value.

But while the idea is simple and powerful, the execution can be considerably complex and sometimes frustrating. Even a cursory consideration of the issue produces a number of thorny questions: How do I know how much of my revenue is leaking? What tools do I need to capture it? How do I manage the inevitable change that will occur in my organization? What types of initiatives should I pursue, and what should be their scope and size?

PricewaterhouseCoopers partners Randy Browning and Sammy Kumar have spent a significant part of their careers answering these questions and working with companies to analyze revenue leakage, and to develop and implement practical strategies to plug those leaks. They have crystallized and distilled the lessons they have learned and the knowledge they have acquired into this book. They know that lost revenue can be identified and then systematically and successfully captured. In this comprehensive book, they:

- Present a framework for understanding revenue leakage within the context of a strong business case.
- Describe the strategies and tactics that underlie the

authors' unique identify-quantify-capture approach.
- Discuss the day-to-day processes into which revenue maximization must be embedded in order to succeed.
- Analyze the advantages and disadvantages of sometimes confusing alternatives among available automated tools.
- Suggest a number of quantifiable monitoring mechanisms that will ensure the revenue maximization strategy stays on track.

The authors also explore what it means to be a revenue-responsible organization and what a company needs to do to get there.

Achieving the optimum balance between theory and practice, the book makes liberal use of real-life examples culled from the authors' experience and from that of their colleagues at PricewaterhouseCoopers. A unique feature of the book is a series of action steps for companies that appear at the conclusion of key chapters. Using these, a company can get started immediately on revenue maximization initiatives.

Aimed at top executives, the book is of equal interest to a broad business audience. Because, ideally, revenue maximization should be an enterprise-wide effort, managers at all levels need to understand the strategies and tactics presented in this book. Since the potential benefits are so great, revenue maximization should be widely understood and put into practice throughout the company. The information contained in this book can help make that happen.

GREG GARRISON
Americas Assurance and Business Advisory Services Leader
PricewaterhouseCoopers

Acknowledgments

This book is the result of a team effort. We could not have written it without the insights, experiences, and hard work of dozens of people who were generous with their time and energy. Our gratitude is immeasurable.

First we would like to thank the corporate executives who took time to talk to us about their experiences with revenue maximization: Terry Mosey, Peter Varley, Mike McGrath, and Ann Sado at Bell Canada; Rick Smith at Eschelon; Tom Berry and Ellyce Brenner at AT&T; Karin Wagar at Verizon; Jeannette Alberte at SBC; Pat Walker at Qwest; Steve Kloeblen at IBM; Alexander Cibenko at St. Vincent's Health Systems; David Buckel and Barbara Gibson at Interland; Susan Cole and Ed Barnes at Pegasus Solutions; Jim Eyster; Rich LaPerch at Vibrant Solutions; Chuck Crenshaw at Connexn Technologies; and Susan McNeice and Jeff Sklaver at TeleStrategies. We also thank several other executives we interviewed who preferred to go unnamed, along with all the clients over the past five years that have inspired us to continue improving and expanding our collection of revenue maximization solutions.

We would next like to thank our PricewaterhouseCoopers colleagues serving other industries for sharing their insights and expertise: David Harris in healthcare; Michael Hurle and Ed Tobia in utilities; Shyam Vendkat, Tim Ryan, and Miles Everson in financial services; Bjorn Hanson in hospitality. We would also like to thank all of our colleagues in our own global InfoComm Advisory Services practice for their creativity, thoughtfulness, sweat, and dedication in helping to perfect revenue maximization strategies and tactics. Although all 300 professionals in the practice deserve to be mentioned and thanked by name, we only have space here to express our gratitude to a few. Most notably, we want to single out Luke Sayers, who was there with us from the start, and Chris Snyder, who supported us from the beginning of building our practice. We also want to express our appreciation to Don Almeida, Greg Garrison, Mitch Cohen, Bill Cobourn, Randy O'Hare, Russ Sapienza, Shelly Slack and Kathy Garlasco for their support and encouragement.

In writing this book, we relied on the help of many people. We want to thank Joel Kurtzman and Mark Friedlich for providing valuable guidance from the firm's global thought leadership team. Thanks also to Gene Zasadinski for his careful and thorough editing.

We especially want to thank the people of The Maloney Group for all their help: in particular, Toni Maloney, Amy Ward Kaup, Joe Chmielewski, and finally, The Maloney Group's "director of writing services" for their hard work, dedicated enthusiasm and commitment to revenue maximization and PwC.

ACKNOWLEDGMENTS

We also want to give exceptional thanks to Sally Potts, for her insights and energetic management throughout the writing, editing, and publishing process.

Finally, on a personal note, Sammy would like to thank the partners he has worked for—and with—over the years, the many members of his team that make us successful everyday, and his family for their love and support. Randy would like to thank his family for their love and support and for putting up with the travel and long hours. He would also like to thank the many colleagues and clients that have inspired him over the years. We owe you all more than we can say for your patience and support.

RANDY BROWNING
SAMMY KUMAR

Contents

INTRODUCTION 1
Why Revenue Maximization?

CHAPTER 1 17
The Value Propositions:
Growth, Profitability, and Integrity

CHAPTER 2 37
Six Facts About Revenue Leakage

CHAPTER 3 45
Three Causes of Revenue Leaks

CHAPTER 4 71
What Companies Are Doing Now

CHAPTER 5 93
Keys to Success: Managing a Revenue
Maximization Initiative

Chapter 6 .... **113**
What a Company Can, Can't, and Should Do Itself

Chapter 7 .... **119**
Day-to-Day Processes

Chapter 8 .... **145**
Key Automated Tools

Chapter 9 .... **175**
The Revenue Responsible Organization

Chapter 10 .... **205**
Quantifiable Monitoring Mechanisms

Chapter 11 .... **223**
Identify, Quantify, Capture

Conclusion **243**
Revenue Maximization Today, Revenue Maximization Tomorrow

Index **249**

Introduction

Why Revenue Maximization?

At a company holiday party in 1998 or 1999, if an executive mentioned a headline initiative that could grow topline revenue by 2 or 3 percent, people probably wouldn't have taken much notice. They would have asked each other why she was so excited, why she was talking so loudly. We lived then in an age of 20 percent annual revenue growth, mega mergers, technology revolutions, and infinite possibility. Dealmakers ran the companies, and operating executives were lost in the shuffle.

Today, if that executive mentioned a 2 or 3 percent topline growth initiative, heads would turn and necks would crane. And if she, feeling more confident, announced that the initiative usually returned three or four times investment, and didn't face any competitor challenges, the music would stop, a spotlight would appear, and a path would clear. People would listen.

We believe that revenue maximization is such an initiative. **It is a proactive strategy—more precisely, a holistic group of strategies—to grow topline revenue, increase profitability, and strengthen corporate integrity by ensuring that a company efficiently captures, in cash, all the revenue it deserves and only the revenue it deserves for the services it provides.** In many industries, where revenue and profit growth have become painfully harder to secure, revenue maximization is one of the most attractive strategies available. And it is the only growth strategy we're aware of that, in the natural course of the initiative, improves a company's credibility with customers and investors.

Revenue maximization is closely related to initiatives like revenue assurance, as it's called in the telecom industry (where our work has been concentrated), and revenue cycle enhancement, as it's called in healthcare and elsewhere. At its core lies a basic accounting textbook concept: the collection of revenue should be timely, accurate, and complete—timely in collecting revenue when it's supposed to be collected; accurate in correctly charging every customer call for every service provided; and complete in collecting revenue for such services. Revenue maximization can also eliminate inefficiencies and process flaws that prevent the incremental sale of services.

But, revenue maximization goes beyond some control-oriented strategies that merely attempt to assure, passively, that revenue collection is timely, accurate, and complete. It makes revenue collection timely, accurate, and complete by systematically and proactively eliminating instances when it's not, instances that cost companies real money, instances that can severely damage corporate integrity.

THE VALUE PROPOSITIONS

In this book, we pound the drums of **growth, profitability,** and **integrity**—the three core value propositions of revenue maximization and three of the primary goals of any enterprise.

First, revenue maximization meets shareholders' primary demand—to significantly grow real earnings. Revenue maximization is a strategy about collecting more cash for services already provided by combating profit-damaging revenue leakage. The opportunities available—the opportunities *within* companies—are substantial, between 2 to 5 percent of total revenue or more in many of the service-sector industries that we focus on in this book.

Second, revenue maximization projects, independent of their aggregate impact, increase profits. The projects are, for the most part, high-return, low-risk, and quantifiable. Because of these high returns and low risk, they provide even more benefits on the bottom line than the top line.

Finally, and especially relevant in the post-Enron world, revenue maximization improves the integrity of customer relationships and financial reporting. In *Building Public Trust*, Robert Eccles and Samuel DiPiazza, the CEO of PricewaterhouseCoopers, detail the key elements of corporate honesty and public trust: a spirit of transparency, a culture of accountability, and people of integrity.[1] A crucial element of corporate integrity is a *commitment to accuracy*, a commitment to substantive tactics to ensure the complete and accurate collection of revenue, a commitment pursued in the natural course of events by companies actively maximizing revenue.

THREE OBJECTIONS

When we told some of our colleagues that we were writing this book, they voiced three objections. First, they told us that revenue maximization is unnecessary because most companies are already doing these "types of things" anyway. Yes, some companies we discuss in this book are ensuring that they get most of the revenue they deserve, and we draw lessons from these leading enterprises. (Though most of these companies don't call their strategies "revenue maximization.") If the world were perfect, revenue leakage wouldn't exist, and you would be reading something else right now. But, globally, companies are leaking revenue from lost transactions, from process inefficiencies, from human error, from system glitches. Companies are leaking revenue because they are unaware of leaks and, frankly, because they tolerate it. They are also leaking revenue because of the pressures that have accelerated the pace of change in most industries—pressures from new products, new technologies, new competitors, new acquisitions, and pressures from earnings growth objectives that forced companies to try to grow too big, too fast.

The second objection we heard is that companies can't do anything about revenue leakage. Revenue will leak until the day humanity figures out how to banish human error. Yes, we don't expect any company ever to capture the mythical last penny of deserved revenue or make revenue collection 100 percent accurate, but the second objection is belied by the first. Companies around the globe are proactively maximizing revenue now.

The third objection is that revenue maximization isn't a growth strategy at all. "Real" growth, they maintain, can come only from selling a new product or service to a customer. Sometimes we hide from this objection by referring to revenue maximization in a less controversial way as a "financial opportunity." Other times, however, our response to this objection is firmer and more empirical: some leading companies are not only experiencing topline growth from revenue maximization, they are also treating revenue maximization *no differently* than they treat other growth strategies. They are building into their budgets and strategic plans the incremental dollars (or yen or euros) from revenue maximization activities just as they build in expected revenue gained from a new marketing plan or a product launch.

WHAT'S NEW ABOUT REVENUE MAXIMIZATION?

Some companies (and parts of companies) are now pursuing revenue maximization with a demonstrably new *intensity* and *attitude*, which together make revenue maximization, in our opinion, a demonstrably new and important strategy.

Two friends may play catch in the backyard, call a few pass plays, tackle each other once or twice, even give each other nicknames, but they're not playing football. So too with revenue maximization. Companies have historically conducted isolated projects to make sure revenue collection is timely, accurate, and complete, but these activities have not been carried out with the cohesiveness, leadership, discipline, and intensity necessary to form a truly proactive and productive strategy.

Equally important, revenue maximization—like revenue leakage, revenue assurance and revenue cycle enhancement—can be considered in either of two ways. As Karin Wagar, Executive Director for IT Billing and Revenue Assurance of Verizon, explained, "Those who are just starting out see it as problem solving. Those who are furthest along see it as an opportunity." This difference in attitude is decisive. We have long used the term "revenue assurance" to describe revenue maximization-like activities, and most of those we interviewed (and quote) in this book still use revenue assurance to describe a broad array of activities to address revenue leakage. But we have come to conclude that revenue maximization more accurately describes how companies *should* pursue the necessary strategies—as *seizing opportunities*, not solving problems, as a road to increased profitability, not as a set of disconnected actions that combat fraud, insert controls or improve inefficient systems. Revenue maximization, in the end, is about capturing leaking revenue, efficiencies, and the benefits of improved integrity.

Table 1.1 supplies some context and defines terms related to revenue maximization.

How do you do it?

Revenue maximization can consistently deliver major financial opportunities. But, as this book documents, it takes commitment to pursue strategies energetically enough to create organizational change, improve day-to-day processes, apply technology, and measure progress. And it requires leadership and will. Throughout this book, we share stories of people confronting the oftentimes instinctive, sometimes uncompromising initial resistance to revenue maximization. Revenue maximization "is not something people jump on," as one executive we spoke to put it. "You have to convince them, cajole them, and beg them to do it." To convince them, a company must never position revenue maximization as a strategy to uncover mistakes. Companies must celebrate the financial and reputational value created by the strategy and never imply that someone lost money or damaged integrity in the first place.

Table 1.1
Some Overlapping Revenue Maximization Terms

Revenue Maximization	A proactive strategy to grow topline revenue, increase profitability, and strengthen corporate integrity by making sure a company efficiently captures, in cash, all the revenue it deserves and only the revenue it deserves for the services it provides.
Revenue Assurance	Telecom industry term for a broad range of revenue maximization-like activities, including early programs like bill audits.
Revenue Cycle Enhancement	Term used in healthcare and other industries for revenue maximization activities. Tends to have process reengineering focus.
Revenue Integrity	Term used in the airline industry to describe revenue maximization-like activities, with emphasis on yield management. Also occasionally used in the telecom industry to describe the "end state" of revenue assurance as a point when integrity—wholeness—of revenue has been achieved.
Revenue Assurance Management	Term used by a few telecom companies to describe integrated revenue assurance and accounts receivable management, with an emphasis on increasing credits and collections and better managing customer accounts.
Cost Minimization	The sibling of revenue maximization, a strategy to grow earnings by minimizing inflated or inaccurate costs.

Revenue maximization requires broad strategic *and* tactical skills to combat leaks. Information technology (IT) systems are tricky. Processes are entrenched. Cultural barriers are high. Maximizing revenue demands strategic focus at the highest levels of the organization, including the CEO, and technical skills to detect, understand, correct, and prevent revenue leakage at a detailed, individual level: individual telephone call records, individual gas meters, individual airline agents. As Pat Walker, Executive Director of Finance Revenue and Operations Treasury at Qwest, told us, "What they say about politics, I say about revenue assurance: All revenue assurance is local." Revenue maximization is, in its simplest terms, a strategy to operate the company better. Through the details of a company's operations, it can capture the major opportunities within.

Whatever its difficulties, a rigorous, determined revenue maximization strategy can be exhilarating. It is also undeniable, as those who've done it can tell you, that searching for leaks forensically through mounds of data, finding real money, and immediately contributing to the bottom line can actually be fun.

Strategic overview

Revenue maximization can be an exhilarating strategy. But it's also one that is difficult to implement and hard to sustain.

We have developed a strategic framework for the methodical, and relentless forward march needed for the initiative to be successful. We believe that four separate strategies are necessary, although we are loath to call them separate strategies because, in fact, they work best—and, in some cases, only work—when executed holistically as illustrated in Figure 1.1. The strategies are:

1. Integrate revenue maximization into all of a company's day-to-day processes
2. Implement key automated tools
3. Create a revenue responsible organization
4. Bond and embed these strategies with quantifiable monitoring mechanisms

Figure 1.1
The Four Core Strategies of Revenue Maximization

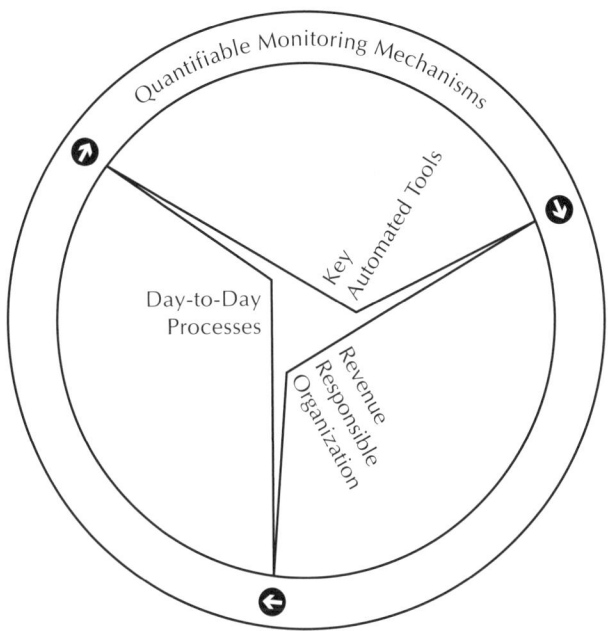

1. **Integrate revenue maximization into all of a company's day-to-day processes.** With clear, measured, and accountable day-to-day processes, companies can prevent root causes of revenue leakage and ensure consistent revenue maximization in a rapidly changing business environment.
2. **Implement key automated tools.** Companies can quantify and capture leaked revenue and improve the accuracy of revenue collection with leading-edge detective, analytical, and preventive tools that are a living part of a company's operations.
3. **Create a revenue responsible organization.** With the right leadership, culture, accountabilities, and struc-

ture, companies can foster an organization that is intolerant of revenue leakage and committed to maximizing revenue.

4. **Bond and embed these strategies with quantifiable monitoring mechanisms.** Companies can use simple, tiered, and continuously adjusted monitoring mechanisms to achieve a best-practice, integrated revenue maximization strategy.

In other words, to maximize revenue, companies need to make positive steps in their processes and their organizations and intelligently use tools and metrics. While we developed this strategic framework for the telecom industry, our research in preparation for this book has convinced us that they will equally enable companies in other industries to seize the opportunities that revenue maximization offers.

To manage the implementation of these core strategies, we have developed the "identify, quantify, capture" approach. We think of the four strategies—tools, processes, organization, and metrics—as the ingredients of a successful revenue strategy. Identify, quantify, capture is the recipe— our add, mix, and bake. Companies we have worked with have achieved success by systematically following the three recipe steps:

- **Identify** where the company or division is leaking and the best revenue capture opportunities.
- **Quantify** how much the company is leaking, the precise causes of that leakage, and the ROI of a program to capture the revenue.
- **Capture** revenue immediately and with preventive capture initiatives.

The identify-quantify-capture approach works on both a macro and micro level as a way to organize an enterprisewide revenue maximization push and as a way to manage individual projects.

Haven't I met you somewhere before?

Revenue maximization may have a familiar ring to some. Like Six Sigma (and Total Quality Management before it), revenue maximization is focused on an enemy—"variation" or "defects" in Six Sigma, leakage in revenue maximization—and proposes cross-functional process, technology, organizational, and quantification strategies to combat that enemy. But there are differences. For example, revenue maximization requires less statistical rigor. Some companies perform revenue maximization activities under the heading of Six Sigma or process improvement. GE's lighting division, for example, used Six Sigma techniques to repair billing problems with Wal-Mart.[2]

There is also, potentially, a difference in scope. Revenue maximization *can* succeed as a Six Sigma-like "mega strategy," but it can also succeed as a "smart strategy," a series of focused projects rather than a central organizing principle of a company. Even if it is not completely implemented, revenue maximization can have a positive impact. (It can even have a positive impact if it's not executed all that well.)

However, while many companies have achieved important gains from a narrower pursuit of revenue maximization, major gains, we believe, are available to those who pursue it as a megastrategy, or as what GE's former CEO Jack Welch refers to more prosaically as an initiative. Welch writes that Six Sigma was one of the most important initiatives of his career. "We defined an initiative as something that grabs everyone," he explains, "large enough, broad enough, and generic enough to have a major impact on the company. An initiative is long lasting, and it changes the fundamental nature of the organization."[3] Companies pursuing revenue maximization as a "Welchian" initiative, use it to concentrate focus on the core missions of the business—shareholder value, quality, integrity, growth.

A few final words about this book

We wrote this book to explain the causes of revenue leakage, to share what companies are now doing right and doing wrong, to describe near- and long-term, actionable best-practice strategies, to make clear the value propositions of revenue maximization, and maybe most important, to convey our enthusiasm for revenue maximization.

This book is not based on a research project. While we did perform research and conducted dozens of interviews with corporate executives and our colleagues at PricewaterhouseCoopers, this book was mainly forged in our personal experience; living, wrestling and succeeding with revenue maximization, applying revenue maximization strategies, and trying to improve and perfect them in the real world. In short, this book is the latest thinking of active practitioners.

We've both spent our careers serving the telecom industry, and in the last five years, both of us have dedicated much of our time, as tactical and strategic advisors, to revenue maximization initiatives in telecom and related industries. In this book, we share our own experiences and draw on the experience, wisdom, and insight of our colleagues around the world helping telecom companies maximize revenue.

A FEW FINAL WORDS ABOUT THIS BOOK

We also expanded the scope of this book to include similar *service-sector* industries—industries with high volumes of transactions, with a high number of different types of transactions, and a high complexity of rates for those transactions. (If a construction firm only sells eight oil rigs a year, it tends to keep track of the bills.) To do this, we consulted our colleagues to learn from them the big-picture issues concerning revenue maximization in the airlines, utilities, cable and direct broadcast satellite (DBS), healthcare, Web services, hospitality, and financial services industries. Many of the strategies and principles in this book also apply to the retail and manufacturing sectors, both in their core businesses and (in the case of manufacturing) the increasingly important service components of their business. However, those sectors are generally outside the book's scope.

We have found that some industries—financial services, for instance—are already forcefully addressing revenue leakage and have already minimized the potential damage from leakage and inaccurate revenue collection. But for some companies in those industries and for most companies in many others, revenue maximization isn't yet, in our opinion, where it should be among competing corporate priorities.

Because our work is concentrated in the telecom industry, many of the projects and real-world examples discussed in this book come from the telecom industry. Obviously, we are most comfortable drawing upon our own experience. We do genuinely believe, though, that the telecom industry is particularly illustrative of revenue maximization for the purposes of this book. In the last five years, the industry has gone through most of the revenue maximization (or revenue assurance) lifecycle, from a point when most companies have never heard of it to a point now when some companies or divisions rank it among their top priorities.

(Analysts at Gartner Dataquest recently reported that, "Revenue assurance has replaced CRM and customer care as the new buzzword for telcos."[4])

All the real-world examples are used not as subjects, but as lessons that demonstrate general principles irrespective of industry and provide guidance on employing the best strategies and avoiding the worst pitfalls. We expect this book to be of slightly more interest to executives in industries, like telecom, that have already begun to focus on revenue leakage. Yet, our mission here is to write a book for all executives in service-sector industries looking for a way to increase the bottom line.

Almost every executive we talked to about this book reminded us that there are no silver bullets in revenue maximization. The challenges are hard—though hardly impossible—and require diligence. This book can only share lessons and advice to meet those challenges. It can't inculcate will. Jeannette Alberte, Assistant Vice President of Customer Billing Operations (and a leading revenue maximization proponent) at SBC, warned us not to encourage readers to fall into the "seven habits" trap in which readers come to a book and expect, after finishing it, to have picked up seven new habits and to have become highly effective people. The act of reading this book will not maximize any revenue. We hope, though, that this book will convince readers that the strategies of revenue maximization are needed and that the challenges can be met. Because the rewards are great.

Notes

1. Samuel A. DiPiazza Jr. and Robert G. Eccles, *Building Public Trust: The Future of Corporate Reporting* (New York: John Wiley, 2002), 7.

2. Peter S. Pande, Robert P. Neuman, and Roland R. Cavanagh, *The Six Sigma Way: How GE, Motorola, and Other Top Companies Are Honing Their Performance* (New York: McGraw-Hill, 2000), 5.

3. John F. Welch, Jr., *Jack: Straight from the Gut* (New York: Warner Business Books, 2001), 298.

4. Norbert Scholz, "Revenue Assurance Providers to Rescue Ailing Telcos," (Stamford, CT: Gartner Dataquest, August 2002), 2.

CHAPTER ONE

THE VALUE PROPOSITIONS: GROWTH, PROFITABILITY, AND INTEGRITY

O ut of all the North American telecom giants, Bell Canada, in particular its Bell Ontario business unit, has probably sweated the most to achieve revenue maximization. Mike McGrath, vice president of Bell Ontario's small and medium enterprises market, formerly ran Ontario's consumer business, the first area in the company to see real gains from revenue maximization strategies. Mike is one of the most articulate and passionate proponents of revenue maximization that we know.

Mike likes to tell a story of his experience last year at a telecom industry revenue assurance conference in London. At the conference, he was fascinated—in a horror-struck way—as speaker after speaker shared tales of misery and woe. Mike recalls one sad sack in particular, a somewhat congested revenue maximization executive, who spent a half hour bellyaching that he couldn't get any attention from anyone in his company because of competing priorities, wariness of yet another new initiative, and his own lack of status.

As the group therapy session continued, Mike grew impatient. Finally, when it was his turn to speak, inspiration hit him, and he put aside his prepared remarks. "I'm going to play two roles here," he announced. He assumed a meek, mousy, nasal tone. "First role. Ladies and gentlemen, we're gathered today to talk about fraud, internal controls, and why we are leaking revenue. And I've brought along a list of 23 obstacles to doing anything about this." Mike's voice returned to normal. "Second role. Ladies and gentlemen, we're here today because I've got a growth initiative to help us grow an additional 2 percent on our revenue target next year. We can do it with little investment. In fact, it would cost five times less than similar-returning initiatives. We can also do it without facing external customer issues." Mike looked around the room. "Now, ladies and gentlemen, which role gets you more excited?"

While the audience didn't run out of the room, jump on the next flight, and storm into their corporate headquarters, taking no prisoners on behalf of revenue maximization, Mike's role-playing did get them more excited. His second role perfectly captures the core value propositions of revenue maximization. As Figure 1.2 illustrates, the strategy creates value in three primary ways:

Figure 1.2
Value Propositions of Revenue Maximization

- **Growth:** Revenue maximization strategies meet shareholders' first demand—to significantly grow real, cash earnings.
- **Profitability:** Individual revenue maximization projects are high-return, low-risk projects with quantifiable bottom line results.
- **Integrity:** Revenue maximization improves the integrity of customer relationships and financial reporting.

Taken together, these, in our mind, make revenue maximization almost irresistible.

PROPOSITION #1: GROWTH

When, with somewhat false naiveté, we asked Ellyce Brenner, Director of Local Product Management at AT&T, what's the point was of pursuing revenue maximization, Ellyce replied, "Clearly, the ongoing financial benefits. Obviously, I think there is a big value prop for establishing revenue assurance at even a well-run operation." In today's challenging economic environment, nearly every company is struggling more than ever to grow the bottom line. (In the last two years, in most industries, the most successful companies have often been the ones that have seen their revenue shrink less.) In good times and bad, revenue maximization provides a *significant* positive revenue and earnings impact to companies that forcefully and comprehensively apply the key strategies. Leaders in embracing the initiative realize that shareholders, analysts, and boards of directors will no longer forgo the opportunity to capture 2 to 5 percent—or more—of revenue because revenue leakage is a "cost of doing business" (or more accurately, an unknown cost of doing business). Nor will they forgo the earnings growth opportunity, which is even greater than the revenue opportunity because of the high returns of revenue maximization projects. Boards and shareholders, we believe, should turn red in anger if they find out that this kind of opportunity isn't being actively pursued at their companies.

Mike McGrath became passionate about revenue maximization because it delivered revenue growth at Bell Canada. The initiative grew revenue by C$67 million *only one year* after the company launched a formal revenue maximization program.[1] Mike recounted that in the pioneering Bell Ontario unit, he and other unit executives felt the normal management and shareholder pressures to grow this business by a certain amount in 2001. When he surveyed his opportunities, he realized that revenue maximization could provide a significant part of that growth. In 2002, the initiative expanded even further. As Terry Mosey, the president of Bell Ontario, told us, "We looked at our plans for 2002 and realized that revenue assurance is our most profitable revenue-generating program, bar none."

Other companies, divisions, and units in other industries have seen even greater growth by capturing one of two kinds of leaks that blight the top line:

- **Direct leaks**, in which the full value of a good or service provided is not collected.
- **Opportunity leaks**, in which process flaws, suboptimal use of assets, or systems inefficiencies stop a company from capturing incremental revenue opportunities.

Most of the leaks discussed in this book are direct leaks—a cable company not charging a customer the full price for premium cable, a telecom company not recording calls for billing purposes. Revenue maximization projects create value by capturing direct leaks immediately and by preventing leaks from happening in the first place. Other projects minimize opportunity leakage. In the airline industry, for example, yield management improvement initiatives, among other goals, stop the opportunity leakage from no-shows and duplicate ticketing. *Air Transport World* reports that no-shows alone cost airlines an average 1.6 percent of annual revenue (which would represent over $200 million at Delta Air Lines, for instance).[2]

We can't emphasize enough that capturing these leaks has nothing to do with reported revenue versus real revenue. Revenue maximization is not an accounting strategy. It is a strategy about *cash*, about collecting, in the door, more money from customers for services already provided. It is capturing the opportunities within.

Capturing 2 to 5 percent or more

In many service-sector industries, the opportunity available in revenue maximization is striking. Globally, revenue leakage costs, not millions, but billions of dollars. We have estimated for at least 5 years that the telecom industry leaks, in general, between 2 to 5 percent of revenue, if not more.

Companies have confirmed this. When we took an interactive poll of 70 telecom companies at an industry conference held in 2000, 28 percent of respondents thought their companies leaked between 2 to 5 percent of revenues. Another 42 percent thought their companies leaked *more* than 5 percent. Only 8 percent of companies estimated that they leaked less than 2 percent.[3]

As detailed in Table 1.2, many of our colleagues working with other sectors estimate similar or higher amounts of leakage. They have also confirmed that, as in the telecom industry, the level of leakage has increased over the past five years in other industries as many of the temporal causes of leakage that we discuss in Chapter 3—M&A activity, for example, or the accelerated pace of new product launches—have become more intense.

Table 1.2
Estimated Revenue Leakage as Percentage of Total Revenue in Selected Service-Sector Industries

Industry	Leakage	Major Leakage Issues
Airlines	2%–5%	Boarding/lift collection, yield management
Cable and DBS	1%–3%	New technology transaction capture, discounts and promotions
Financial Services	1%–2%	Little direct leakage
Healthcare	5%–10%	Insurer/government payment collection, accounts receivable aging, charge capture
Hospitality	1%–2%	Little direct leakage
Telecom	2%–5%+	Service provisioning, intercarrier relationships, unreconciled systems
Utilities	2%–5%	Unbilled meters, outdated billing systems, unreconciled systems
Web Services	5%–10%	Inaccurate provisioning, poor usage measurement, poor service integrity

Although we doubt that few companies nowadays would explicitly reject a 2 to 5 percent revenue growth initiative—even one that might take several years to seize—it is interesting to note the relative magnitude of this opportunity. A recent Credit Suisse First Boston report calculated that real annual sales growth from 1992-2001 was only 7.4 percent for American companies with revenue over $500 million, not the double-digit growth of people's imagination.[4] This growth rate includes revenue from acquisitions. And this was during the largest economic expansion in history.

Today many industries are scrambling to find any source of revenue growth. *The Economist* reported that despite traffic growth in the global telecom industry, "The industry has found to its cost [that] traffic growth does not translate into revenue growth. Moreover, in the rich world at least, markets are saturated. So new revenue cannot come from new subscribers either."[5] The author argued that new revenue must come from new services to existing subscribers.

We argue that it can also come from revenue maximization.

Interestingly, many of the companies now exerting little effort to maximize revenue don't explicitly reject the opportunity. They just, for the most part, don't see it. Revenue leakage usually doesn't mean that hundred-dollar bills are falling out of a hole in the CEO's old suit pants or that a single IT system is leaking five percent of a company's total revenue. True, companies occasionally suffer acute life-or-death revenue leakage. In the early 1990s, for example, at one of the major U.S. long-distance providers, a faulty and leaky billing system almost brought the company down. More recently, many competitive local exchange carriers (CLECs) that arose to compete with the incumbent Baby

Bells experienced severe, and, in some cases, terminal revenue leakage. Similarly, in the healthcare industry, our colleagues have frequently worked with hospital organizations where leakage was threatening to destroy an organization's total financial health. But for most companies, leakage is more akin to sluggishness or death by a thousand cuts. A robust maximization strategy creates value by accreting many small- and medium-sized gains, pennies, and dollars multiplied by thousands of customers and millions of transactions.

Where's the proof?

The proof is woven throughout this book: individual projects and individual companies achieving success and capturing millions of dollars by maximizing revenue. The team we lead has quantified well over US$1 billion in revenue maximization opportunities in the telecom industry alone. (We've only, we believe, scratched the surface.) Our clients are now capturing much of this. Our colleagues serving utilities, cable, and healthcare industries report similar sizable value creation. But, sadly for the skeptics, much of the proof is difficult to document for two reasons. First, companies themselves usually won't go on record about what they've done for competitive or legal reasons. Executives we've spoken to are eager to spread the joys of revenue maximization, but they're not so eager to spread inside information. Confidentiality agreements prevent outside advisors like us from discussing completed projects too specifically. Second, *much of the success in revenue maximization is still to come.* We are confident that leading telecom companies, for instance, will achieve 4 or 5 percent revenue growth when they fully implement the necessary revenue maximization strategies.

So how do we make people believers? We can talk about growth through maximization until we're blue in the face, or as Tom Berry, Director of Revenue Assurance Management at AT&T, said to us, we can let the process happen. Tom noted, "When people work hard and miss their numbers and begin to understand that there are tens of millions of dollars in leakage, if not hundreds of millions, then they become believers."

Proposition #2: profitability

The second value proposition of revenue maximization—the *profits* created by the quantifiable high return on investment (ROI) of individual revenue maximization projects—both complements and diverges from the first. It complements the first because the impact of revenue maximization, due to its high returns, relatively low investment, and low risk, is proportionally greater on the earnings line than the revenue line. (In other words, revenue maximization increases operating margins and corporate profitability.) The value proposition diverges because revenue maximization projects should be conducted not only because of the magnitude of the total opportunity—"I'm not doing this unless it gets me 5 percent"—but also because individual projects create real profits and real value and make companies more profitable, more productive, and lower-cost competitors.

The greater return of revenue maximization is simple arithmetic. Telecom giant SBC, for example—we selected it at random—earned about $8 billion in 2001 on $54 billion in revenue. If revenue maximization added only 2 percent to the revenue line over two or three years and—conservatively—0.5 percent to the expense line (since the 300 percent ROI initiatives didn't demand full incremental investment), the company would add 7.6 percent to its net earnings. Assuming SBC's price-to-earnings ratio remained constant, the 7.6 percent earnings growth would boost the company's market capitalization by over $6 billion.

THE RETURNS ARE HIGH

In our experience and in that of those executives we consulted before writing this book, the rough mean of ROI projects is 300 percent in the first year. The first projects companies pursue can be much higher. Revenue maximization shakes bushels of low-hanging fruit off the tree, and we have worked on many projects that exceeded 10 times investment. We have worked on projects exceeding 40 times investment. We have never seen a project fail to breakeven in the first year. As Rich LaPerch, CEO of Vibrant Solutions, a revenue assurance software developer for the telecom industry, told us, "Every company talks about three to six month ROI, and we're meeting that. This is the first industry I've ever been involved in where we're always succeeding in meeting the payback period. We can show 30 or 40 examples of this. Even our 'failures' are successes by anyone else's measures."

The high returns cross a number of industries:

- A British Airways executive reported that the company generates up to $93 million annually from a half-million-dollar annual investment in "revenue integrity," much of it from a longstanding yield management program to capture opportunity leakage.[6]

PROPOSITION #2: PROFITABILITY 27

- New Jersey's Capital Health Systems, according to an article in *Healthcare Financial Management*, has increased cash flow by $30 million, increased patient service revenue by 7 percent, and achieved a return on investment of 10 to 1 in a broad multidisciplinary accounts receivable recovery and revenue enhancement program.[7]

- Projects at Bell Canada, in its first two years of its robust revenue maximization program, returned 5 to 20 times investment in the first year completed. The company captured revenue in a broad array of activities, including minimizing unsubstantiated billing adjustments by customer care people, correcting areas where the company was not billing for services entitled, altering unrealistic winback and lapsed promotional programs, and implementing better controls on the rate tables used to generate bills.

THE INVESTMENTS ARE LOW AND SO IS THE RISK

The profits generated by revenue maximization projects have as much to do with the ROI of the projects' denominators as with their numerators. They simply don't cost much. The opportunities are *within* the company—the revenue has already been "earned" by providing the underlying services—and capturing the opportunities doesn't demand the marketing, development, or major equipment costs of other initiatives. Yes, revenue maximization requires cash outlays, mainly for technology tools and occasional outside expertise. Most often, the bulk of the investment is employees' time.

Importantly, revenue maximization often doesn't require incremental resources. Almost all companies have people dedicated to billing assurance, financial assurance, or other control-oriented activities. Many companies have hundreds of workers manually processing what are essentially revenue leaks: for instance, rejected claims from insurance or government payers at hospitals or call records rejected by billing systems at telecom companies. A robust revenue maximization strategy will allow "efficiency capture," eliminating the need for much of the manual leak processing, identifying redundancies when this manual checking does little good, or redeploying people to become revenue maximizers. As one revenue assurance executive told us, with a more robust strategy, "We get away from the auditor role. We become analysts."

On a risk-adjusted basis, revenue maximization projects stack up even better. Obviously, the projects, as most do, face occasional unforeseen problems. Returns don't always meet expectations, especially in the early, fledgling stages of a program. Yet, comparatively speaking, revenue maximization projects pose few risks:

- They are *little affected by external factors*: competitor action, customer demand, or the economy.
- They are *scaleable* and can be done in measured stages, so cash outlays and employee assignments are easily reversed or canceled.
- They almost *never adversely affect* the business.

Other than a risk to an individual's reputation if a strategy fails, the only serious risk in revenue maximization is the possibility of wasting people's time. But even that risk is small, we believe. For, even if a company launches and abandons a revenue maximization project, it has still at least temporarily addressed efficiency and effectiveness issues and has still bolstered corporate integrity in better assuring itself that it is actually capturing the revenue it earns and only the revenue it earns.

Quantifiable Returns

Chief among the ways revenue maximization differentiates itself as a new strategy is the centrality of quantification in all aspects of the initiative. Companies do—and must—quantify the benefits and investment of revenue maximization. Even earlier, companies must apply tactics to quantify sources and magnitude of revenue leakage. Just as Six Sigma depends on hard quantification strategies through rigorous statistical methods, revenue maximization strategies depend on sampling and extrapolation techniques. Best practice revenue maximization is not simply a process of "fixing something," scratching one's head, wondering how much money the project brought in, and wondering whether or not it was all, in the end, really worth it.

Proposition #3: Integrity

If shareholders and the public are demanding anything nowadays more loudly than revenue growth and profitability, it's honesty. While revenue maximization won't eliminate corporate misdeeds, the strategy will *improve the integrity of customer bills and reported revenue.* The same strategies that tackle human errors, systems glitches, and process flaws and, in general, make sure that revenue collection is accurate, uncover cases where it's not, regardless of who ultimately benefits. These strategies return corporate focus, as it should be, to the fundamentals of operations and management.

In many projects we've worked on, we've found noteworthy instances of overbilling and overprovisioning of services. It's a serious and prevalent problem in many industries. For example, Rick Smith, President of Eschelon, a CLEC operating mainly in the western United States, told us that in the telecom industry, "A really well-run finely tuned billing system might be inaccurate by 3 or 4 percent. A poorly-run, poorly-assembled billing system might have errors of 20 to 25 percent." (Errors include over- and underbilling.) However inadvertent—and in our experience, it's almost always inadvertent—overbilling (either because the price billed is inaccurate or the services weren't provided) can seriously damage a company's reputation, credibility, and customer relationships. Most ominously, overbilling can bring on regulators, lawsuits, short sellers, and, in some cases, law enforcement. In the U.S. healthcare industry, where the government receives roughly half of all bills, violations of the federal False Claims Act can result in serious consequences, even for clerical errors. Similarly, in early 2001, before its more recent problems, WorldCom paid $88 million in a civil law suit for dropping customers from calling plans and charging them higher "casual caller" rates. Even the plaintiffs' attorney admitted to the *Los Angeles Times* that the errors were not done on purpose. Most of the overcharges were due to minor mistakes in processing orders.[8] A robust revenue maximization strategy would have, in its natural course, averted these mistakes.

Most senior executives, we have found, understand the intangible but crucial value of knowing that reported revenue is timely, accurate, and complete, and that one's company proactively and regularly uses best-practice technology, processes, and strategies to ensure that accuracy and completeness. Major repeated overbilling or overprovisioning of services can cause sizable, embarrassing, and dangerous restatements of earnings. Revenue maximization minimizes the risk that a CEO or CFO will find himself or herself in an editorial cartoon, dressed in stripes (or actually dressed in stripes, given the new SEC requirements for CEOs to personally certify financial statements). That's why we believe there's little downside risk to making initial investments in revenue maximization. As Mike McGrath said to us, "It's a powerful feeling to know that you're really getting all the revenue you're supposed to be getting when you put your head down at night."

THE ASYMMETRY OF INACCURACY

Some companies are suspicious of revenue maximization because they ask, "How can revenue maximization be a major financial opportunity if it corrects overbilling or overprovisioning, corrections that would lower revenue?" One telecom company we know of worried that the effect of revenue maximization and correcting both underbilling and overbilling would net, in sum, in their customers' favor. Its legal department, in a very disturbing example of "hear no evil, see no evil," blocked aspects of a revenue maximization program, lest the company eventually be forced to start offering refunds to all its customers.

Repeated overbilling or overprovisioning does occasionally occur, especially in complicated business-to-business arrangements. But in our experience, nine out of ten revenue maximization projects reveal that *the amount of underbilling is significantly greater than the amount of overbilling*. The explanation is simple. Customers of all businesses have wonderfully asymmetrical eyesight. They can spot an overcharge from 50 yards off but don't manage to notice the undercharges right under their noses. Undercharges thus tend to persist. (Customers will even demand adjustments of one part of a bill that is incorrect in the company's favor and ignore parts of the same bill that are incorrect in the customers' favor.)

Best of both worlds. Revenue maximization gives a company the best of both worlds. By actively making sure that the revenue collected is accurate, it energetically strives to eliminate revenue leakage and increase revenue and profits. By also striving to eliminate overbilling and other errors that lead to overcharging customers, it gives companies the benefits of knowing that it is doing right by those customers. For those not satisfied with "doing right"—and we have seen companies like this—reducing overbilling also produces important, tangible benefits, like allowing companies to save on the enormous resources now spent handling irate customers complaining about bills that are too high. It also minimizes the cost of salespeople spending all their time holding customers' hands and listening to complaints, instead of selling new services. Even when a customer isn't directly involved, the cost of correcting glitches and errors can be enormous. In the healthcare industry, for example, billions are spent by both insurers and providers on re-filing claims, on status inquiries, and on other manual paperwork related to incorrect processing and billing.

Finally, inaccurate bills and the system inefficiencies and glitches that cause them are a frequent cause of customer churn in many industries. (A customer doesn't care if a company net-net leaks revenue. He only cares that only one item on his bill is too high.) Among CLECs, customer churn of 2 percent a month is considered a good rate. Eschelon's Rick

Smith told us, "Poor billing will result in higher customer churn and lower growth. Taken to extremes, it will literally put your company out of business. If churn goes up to 3 or 4 percent a month, you're losing 30 or 40 percent of your customers a year. You can't add sales people fast enough to fight this."

Rick then made an impassioned case for the total value of revenue maximization: "In the environment we're in today, it's very easy to say, 'I can't afford revenue assurance.' But an organization can't afford *not* to do this. I'd be amazed if there was any telecom company that couldn't cost-justify this effort. Once you've done it, it's so easy to cost-justify it's ridiculous."

An added benefit

There is an added benefit to revenue maximization outside the three value propositions. Revenue maximization allows a company to use people more wisely by making employees and managers, who've often been in mistake-prevention roles, active contributors to the enterprise's central mission. "What has given me the biggest charge is to watch people develop and become so enthusiastic about this work effort," Ellyce Brenner told us about the revenue maximization projects she has managed. "People are very excited about the money we're finding. They keep on finding new things to investigate and new things to do." People enjoy finding "lost" money, whether a twenty-dollar bill on the street, a five-dollar bill in an old pair of pants, or $50 million for the company.

We also frequently see the opposite: an invisible frustration that plagues some companies, a sort of chronic fatigue syndrome in which initiatives never seem to be working

34   THE VALUE PROPOSITIONS

right, in which new products or new systems never seem to generate the returns expected. In many cases, this chronic fatigue is a function of chronic leakage.

Revenue maximization also creates enthusiasm and excitement because it is, in a way, a rallying cry for excellence. It pushes people to run their businesses better. Terry Mosey at Bell Ontario has sounded the trumpets for the strategy at his company. "When we were growing rapidly," he explained, "we used to think that if we were capturing 95 percent of revenues from new initiatives, life was great and wonderful. But we are such a volume and velocity business that 1 percent means a huge opportunity to us. We looked in the mirror and asked ourselves, "Are we striving for excellence? Are we going to be satisfied with 95 percent? What are we leaving on the table? Great companies don't leave stuff on the table. Our target should be 99.999 percent."

Notes

1. Bell Canada, "Revenue Assurance: Solving Revenue Mystery Turns Up Big Money," *Bell News*, August 2002 (Toronto: Bell Canada), 6.

2. Joan M. Feldman, "Out the Window," *Air Transport World*, 1 September 2001, 49.

3. PricewaterhouseCoopers, "Interactive Benchmarking: Summary Results from PricewaterhouseCoopers Session at Revenue Assurance 2000," (New York: PricewaterhouseCoopers, 2000), 6.

4. Michael J. Mauboussin and Kristin Bartholdson, "Great (Growth) Expectations," *The Consilient Observer*, (New York: Credit Suisse First Boston, 23 April 2002), 2.

5. "Too Many Debts; Too Few Calls," *The Economist*, 20 July 2002, 6.

6. Feldman, "Out the Window," 49.

7. Timothy Graham, "Increasing Revenue through A/R Recovery," *Healthcare Financial Management*, 1 November 2001, 60.

8. Elizabeth Douglass, "MCI's Parent Will Pay as Much as $88 Million to Settle Lawsuit," *Los Angeles Times*, 13 January 2001, C-1.

CHAPTER TWO

SIX FACTS ABOUT REVENUE LEAKAGE

Revenue assurance and especially revenue maximization are foreign words to many executives. Yet every executive knows about revenue leaks, about operating inefficiencies and errors in specific processes and systems. Every industry is prone to specific leakage points, and many industries have, for years, suffered knowingly and often acquiescently from the same leaks. Most revenue leaks at the transaction level are technical and industry-specific, and we have spared the reader mysterious references to "810 transactions" at electric utilities or "UNE-P" at telecom companies.

Rather, we will focus in this chapter and the next one, broadly, on why companies leak. The reasons are similar across all industries: the same temporal causes, cultural susceptibilities, and proximate causes related to people, processes, and technology. Before we detail the causes of leakage in the next chapter, we make a few preliminary points about the nature of the problem. Six facts clarify the enemy.

1. **Leaks occur in drips and dribbles.** As we mentioned in Chapter 1, revenue leaks are not usually fist-sized, three-percent-of-revenue holes in a single pipe causing metaphoric gushers, flooding metaphoric basements, although occasionally we have seen those. Leakage usually occurs in drips and dribbles. At medium- or large-sized enterprises, however, a single dribble can represent millions of dollars.

2. **Leaks don't always mean mistakes.** Many executives, when first encountering the concept of revenue leakage, take the factual statement, "you're leaking" to be the moral equivalent of "you're lazy." But revenue leakage often happens for understandable and defensible business reasons. Frequently, for example, a sales and marketing function will insist, smartly and rightly, to launch a new service or pricing plan immediately to preserve market share. Because the new service or plan is complicated, the rushed company will often have to cobble together a temporary—and usually leaky—networking or provisioning solution. In one example at a telecom company, customers who took advantage of a famous pricing promotion couldn't be billed for three months because the company had made a conscious decision to go forward, using systems that couldn't handle the new rate structure.

3. **Leaks happen within functions, between functions, and across functions.** One of the great myths of revenue leakage is that because most leaks appear as

SIX FACTS ABOUT REVENUE LEAKAGE

billing errors, faulty billing systems caused the leaks. Billing systems are occasionally at fault, but, more often than not, billing errors are only the symptom. The diseases are everywhere. Figure 2.1 illustrates only *one* of the many potential leaks within functions of the revenue cycles of healthcare and cable and DBS companies.

Figure 2.1
Sample Leaks in Two Industries

Function	Sample Leak	Sample Leak	Function
Healthcare			Cable and DBS
Pre-registration/ Registration	Patient co-payment not collected		
		Incorrect plans or promotions sold to customers	Sales and Marketing
Insurance Verification	Claims denied because incorrect insurance procedures followed		
		Set top boxes not properly provisioned	Installation/ Activation
Charge Capture	Service provider failure to record charge		
		Incomplete capture of pay-per-view events	Transaction Capture
Coding/ Documentation	Incorrect code by coding clerks		
		High level of transactions in suspense	Rating and Invoicing
Billing	Incomplete claims		
		Excessive network outages	Network Infrastructure
Collections/ Insurance Follow-up	Inadequate controls lead to excessive denials		
		Over/underpayment of invoices	Interconnection
Contract Monitoring	Contract complexity leading to underpayment		
		Incomplete information required to bill advertisers	Advertising
Bad Debt Processing	Aging of receivables		
		Excessive customer disputes	Financials

Importantly leaks and, more generally, inaccurate revenue collection, persistently occur *between* functions, as for instance, when a telecom company's or electric utility's network is not properly integrated with a billing system. In a 2001 report, market research firm IDC estimated that 45 percent of all billing-related leaks in the telecom industry happen because of data collection and data mediation issues, 20 percent because of order management issues, 10 percent because of assorted other issues, and only 25 percent because of direct billing (rating and invoicing) issues.[1]

Finally, leaks occur *across* functions, in which cause and effect reside in different areas of the revenue cycle. For example, in the healthcare industry, hospitals sometimes enter into complex managed care contracts with little input from billing or patient financial services areas and with the false expectation that existing staff and IT systems can support the new contracts. These complex contracts end up producing whole categories of payments denied and delayed by the managed care company, requiring heavy (and error-prone) manual reprocessing at the hospitals.[2]

4. **Capturing leaks provides sustainable incremental revenue.** Some executives consider maximizing revenue to be the same as eliminating the corporate yacht: not a bad idea, but hardly a sustainable road to growth. However, like any good growth strategy, revenue maximization offers more than one-time benefits. When a cable company, for example, finally charges a customer the right rate for premium services, the immediate capture of direct leakage in recurring services adds to the company's base. And the preventive cap-

ture of "one-time" leaks—failing to charge for a set of crutches, for instance, or mistakenly not registering an analog electric meter onto the master system—also provides sustainable benefits by establishing processes (or using technology) to maximize the number of crutches and kilowatts accurately and completely billed.

5. **Revenue maximization initiatives will increasingly focus on opportunity leaks.** Throughout this book, we most often discuss direct revenue leakage because that's where most companies have concentrated their efforts so far. Addressing opportunity leakage—leakage that limits incremental revenue—is, we believe, the next significant phase of revenue maximization. For sectors like financial services, in which direct leakage is a small problem, opportunity leakage is the primary focus of revenue maximization-like activities now.

Opportunity leaks occur for as wide a variety of reasons as direct leaks. They happen, for example, because a business rule at a company evolved passively. One wireless telecom company we worked with had inconsistent and outdated corporate rules on rounding the length of calls for billing purposes. Eventually, it captured a major opportunity by rounding all calls to the half-minute, a policy consistent with all of its major competitors. Opportunity leaks frequently occur because assets—airline seats, for example, or telecom network capacity—are not optimized, and new customers are denied new services because of a preventable "belief" that the network is full. Bad or inadequate data cause opportunity leaks in other ways, such as uncoordinated information between sales and operations functions leading to a sales push for the wrong (or unprofitable) products. Opportunity leaks also occur when poor processes create *untimely* collection of revenue and thus the inefficient use of assets, people, or working capital.

6. **Revenue leaks are often interwoven with cost issues.** The suboptimal use of assets behind much opportunity leakage is often seen through another lens, as inefficient costs. Many airlines, for instance, view the empty seats on every plane as *costing* the company a certain amount. Similarly, telecom and utilities companies routinely lose physical assets—circuits and meters are simply nowhere to be found in a company's systems—and a strategy to eliminate costs by preventing wasteful expenditure on assets is the same thing as a strategy to maximize revenue to find these "wasted" assets and use them to generate sales.

Also, it may be a cliché that one person's cost is another person's revenue. In the telecom industry in particular, "intercarrier" leakage issues have exploded in the last five years as companies, especially CLECs and wireless operators, have entered complicated arrangements with other telecom companies on whose networks their calls partly travel. Intercarrier cost and revenue issues can become even more of a stew when companies resell services, as most telecom companies now do. If, for example, a telecom company sells hundreds of dedicated circuits to a customer, a portion of the dedicated circuits might belong to a *third* company. Thus an attempt to maximize profitability involves not only making sure that the customer is paying for all the circuits provided but also making sure that the company is not overpaying costs for the resold third-party circuits.

In our practice, we refer to the cost sibling of revenue maximization as cost minimization. We use the term only to describe cost "leaks," not broad corporate cost-cutting initiatives like reducing headcount. (Unfortunately, there is no good way to describe the mistakes, inefficiencies, and glitches that can cause higher costs. "Bubbles" is too broad. "Protrusions" is too graphic. "Anti-leaks" is too obscure.) Many of the organizational, procedural, and technological strategies we talk about in this book apply equally to cost minimization activities. Many companies don't separate cost minimization from revenue maximization activities. In the cable and DBS industry in particular, companies tend to aggregate cost and revenue issues into a general push for "margin enhancement." All that being said, there are differences between cost and revenue strategies, and in this book, for clarity of purpose, we concentrate primarily on the latter.

NOTES

1. Levant Toros, "Service Provider Revenue Assurance Market Analysis and Trends" (Framingham, MA: IDC, September 2001), 6.

2. Mary Calloe and David Harris, "Managed Care Contracting and PFS" (Westchester, IL: Healthcare Financial Management Association Patient Friendly Billing Project, 2002), 3.

CHAPTER THREE

THREE CAUSES OF REVENUE LEAKS

Many companies often suspect that little green gremlins are behind every revenue leak—"It just doesn't make any sense that these meters weren't turned on"—**but three layers of causality lie underneath every revenue leak, no matter how arbitrary they seem: temporal causes, cultural susceptibilities, and proximate causes.**

The underlying causes of revenue leakage and inaccurate revenue collection, as shown in Figure 3.1, are like the causes of catching a cold. The temporal causes are why this or that virus has come to one's area or why this or that virus is so potent now. The cultural susceptibilities are why an individual is particularly vulnerable to the virus: he hasn't had a drop of Vitamin C since 1972 or, disregarding his wife's advice, he habitually goes outside with his hair still wet. The proximate causes are why he caught this cold now: some creep sneezed on him or his son brought the virus home from school.

Figure 3.1
Three Causes of Revenue Leakage

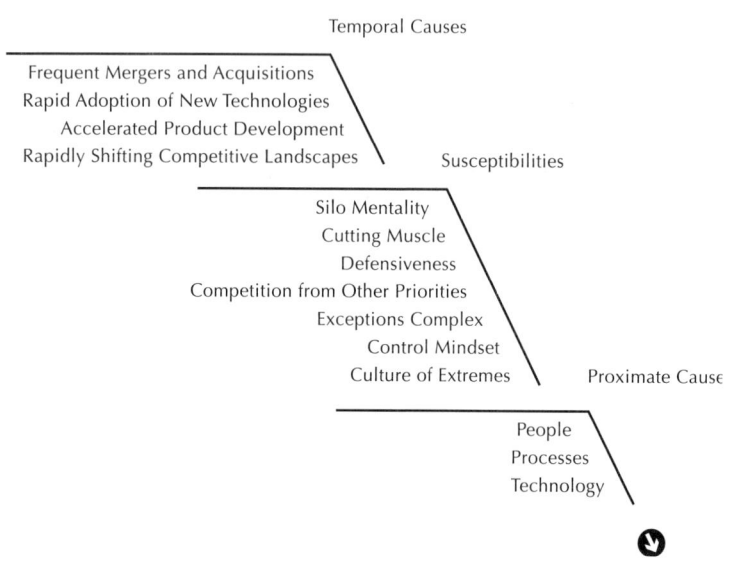

TEMPORAL CAUSES: CHANGE CAUSES LEAKS

While there is probably a Murphy's Law explanation as to why revenue leaks "happen," the rapid pace of change explains why revenue leakage has become an increasingly serious issue during the last five or six years. During that time, every industry has experienced faster and more frequent changes:

TEMPORAL CAUSES: CHANGE CAUSES LEAKS

- Frequent mergers and acquisitions as part of industry consolidation and expansion
- More rapid adoption of new technologies
- Accelerated pace of product development and marketing
- Rapidly shifting competitive landscapes and business models

Attempting to rank the importance of these temporal causes is a futile exercise. Each has led to serious and repeated revenue leakage. Attacking that leakage and making revenue collection more timely, accurate, and complete will help companies improve profitability, integrity, and growth.

FREQUENT MERGERS AND ACQUISITIONS

Mergers may produce synergies in the long term, but in the short term, they are more likely to produce migraines and nervous breakdowns. For instance, trying to reconcile a billing system and a provisioning system is a difficult exercise in itself, but, in the age of frequent mergers, companies must now cope with multiple billing and provisioning systems. Take a company like SBC: Southwestern Bell merged with PacBell, Southern New England Telephone, and Ameritech, and then combined all its wireless assets into a major joint venture, Cingular, with BellSouth. SBC's Chief Information Officer, Edward Glotzbach, explained in 2000 that, "We have 30 different billing systems, each developed a little differently and in a different period of time. It was a big enough problem when we just had one company, but, now that we have multiple companies, we have multiple legacy systems that we have to assimilate into one architecture for the corporation."[1] Even a smaller company like Pegasus Solutions, a provider of technology systems and transaction services to the hospitality industry, faces sizable challenges due to diverse IT systems after a major merger. As Susan Cole, Pegasus' CFO told us, "Any company processing a large number of transactions can be ripe for leakage, especially when multiple legacy systems are linked together. Being pro-active on this front just makes good business sense."

For some companies with decentralized assets, such as those in the utilities, cable, or wireless telecom sectors, frequent acquisitions also lead to new regulatory schemes or new cultures with different revenue assurance approaches and vigor.

Even with unimpeachable due diligence, companies will acquire operations or systems that turn out to be mystifyingly and unexpectedly leaky. A telecom executive told us about quantifying the revenue leaking from one acquisition's network. "The size of the problem really surprised me," she said. "There really weren't any methods or procedures in how they built [the network]—no ground rules. And really good people built it."

The proximate causes (which we talk about at the end of this chapter) of M&A-related revenue leaks include technical issues where, almost literally, revenue falls out of a connecting pipe between a merged company's systems. They also include organizational issues. A few telecom executives related to us frustrations with weakening corporate commitment to revenue maximization after a major merger. "We got it," one executive told us about her company internalizing the importance of the initiative, "and then we lost it, and now we're slowly getting it again."

TEMPORAL CAUSES: CHANGE CAUSES LEAKS

Rapid Adoption of New Technologies

Few companies have had the luxury of writing the head-spinning new technologies of the last few years onto a blank slate of processes and systems. The companies have had to bolt on the new technologies—or, often more accurately, tape and staple them—to existing systems. Many systems, for technical reasons, simply don't work seamlessly together. In other cases, the process of bolting-on new technology requires manual intervention and spawns manual error.

New back-office systems cause leaks. Stories are legion about problems and leaks related to new Enterprise Resource Planning or Customer Relationship Management implementations. *Modern Healthcare* magazine reported on particularly pernicious problems at some hospitals caused by new billing systems. The University of Chicago Hospitals faced a cash crunch, ended the year 6 percent below budget, and was forced to establish a bank line of credit because more than 60 percent of the claims generated by a new billing system for the first two months in operation were either inaccurate or incomplete. Despite this, the organization was one of the lucky ones. Some other hospitals were either forced into bankruptcy or had their credit ratings reduced after financial crises triggered by billing system installations.[2]

New services created by new technology also cause leaks. Many companies are simply not fully prepared or don't have the institutional skills to make sure that, in the initial stages of selling new technology-related services, they are collecting all the revenue to which they are entitled. Cable companies, for example, have faced serious revenue leakage issues—services not being billed correctly or not being billed at all—when offering new, technology-enabled services such as high-speed data, video-on-demand, or telephony services.

The challenges arising from the underlying service-delivery technology have been aggravated by the need to bill many of these services on a per-use basis with systems originally designed to bill monthly recurring charges.

Similarly, in the wireless telecom sector, manufacturers built text-messaging capabilities into second-generation mobile phones. Customers took to this service in unexpected droves (many to complete important tasks like messaging ex-boyfriends, "I H8 U"). Yet some companies did not adequately prepare their systems—called short messaging services centers—for peak traffic and lost considerable revenue because of overloaded conditions.

Accelerated pace of product development and marketing

If all this wasn't enough, companies must bring these new services to market faster. Accelerating competitive pressures and corporate moves to keep share prices up with entries into every new market (such as 3G mobile technology in the telecom industry) force companies to miss control points and skip steps in revenue maximization processes to ensure that companies collect all the revenue and only the revenue they deserve. In the telecom industry, for example, practically without exception, companies quickly going to market with DSL data services faced huge problems in billing and provisioning. It was more of a learning minefield than a learning curve.

Companies are going to market ever faster with products and services unrelated to new technology. In general, as one executive said to us, "New products tend to be complex with lots of packages. The possibility for error is enormous. There are too many human decisions needed in this process, and it is often just too flawed." In the airlines and telecom and, increasingly, the utilities industries, rapid changes in prices and discounts and a spiraling diversity of pricing categories related to new, faster marketing initiatives lead companies to cut corners, plug square pegs into round holes, and make mistakes. More and more, pricing schemes are not truly compatible with existing billing systems. In the telecom industry, "Provisioning people have to jerry-rig contracts into billing systems not capable of dealing with them," one executive told us. "Then they simply turn away from the contracts because they don't want to see what they've wrought."

Rapidly changing competitive landscapes and business models

Finally, most service sectors have undergone a major shift (and sometimes shifts) in the competitive landscape. New suppliers, new customer channels, new regulatory schemes, new competitors, new payers, and more are causing changes that, in turn, cause revenue leakage:

- In the U.S. healthcare industry, managed care and government payers are now, famously, more rigorous in scrutinizing claims, leading to more payment denials and more demands on healthcare providers' systems and processes. As Alexander Cibenko, Vice President of Patient Financial Services at Saint Vincent Catholic Medical Centers of New York, the city's largest Catholic healthcare system, said to us, "The billing processes, the technicalities of the billing process—you need to make sure that you can meet every third-party's data edits and requirements as well as very complex reimbursement algorithms—this was already very, very complicated, intense, and demanding. Now, the environment is even more intense with the addition of rules, edits and reimbursement algorithms...making the whole process even more intense."

- For the telecom and utilities industries in many countries, deregulation has created whole new classes of intercorporate relationships, forcing companies to bill ever more complicated aggregated transactions.

- The convergence of industries has created new sources and types of revenue leakage in companies previously unexposed to leakage issues, such as at retail companies that have acquired media assets, or at media companies that have acquired high volume-transaction Internet operations.

In many industries, recent rapid shifts in the competitive landscape also meant that new competitors—DBS companies, local electricity marketers, CLECs—appeared every day, it seemed, putting tremendous pressure on prices and margins. This forced companies to cut expenses and attack the supposed "cost centers" necessary to proactively pursue revenue maximization.

All this change has had one more important, though indirect, impact on revenue leakage. It has produced, until recently, shareholder growth. Companies didn't focus on revenue leakage because they didn't have to. "Growth can hide a lot of sins," reflected one executive we spoke to. "Big deals can hide a lot of sins." He believed that his company and others simply took their eye off the ball—off of operational diligence, off of being thorough about ensuring that they accurately and completely collect the revenue from the services they sell.

Today, of course, there are far fewer opportunities to hide the sins.

Susceptibilities: the cultural causes

While nearly every company faces the same temporal causes of leakage, not every company leaks the same amount. (That's what makes things interesting.) And some individual companies are simply more susceptible to leakage. In our experience, the most common susceptibilities are:

1. The silo mentality
2. Cutting muscle and the lack of resources
3. Defensiveness
4. Competition from other priorities
5. The exceptions complex
6. The control mindset
7. A culture of extremes

Companies obviously vary in their susceptibilities. (We've seen plenty of companies, though, that suffer from all seven.) In Chapter 9, we return to the issue of cultural causes of leakage when we detail the revenue-responsible organization and specific organizational and cultural features of a revenue-maximizing company. But, in this section, we make the case that many companies leak revenue because, frankly, they allow it to happen.

1. THE SILO MENTALITY

The silo mentality—individuals and corporate functions not thinking outside their own tasks or responsibilities, often because they have no time or incentive to do so—is a common criminal in management books. One can add revenue leakage to the rap sheet. In industry after industry, the silo mentality is not only among the biggest cultural causes of revenue leakage, it is also one of the most common reasons why revenue isn't maximized. Revenue leakage happens across functions and between functions, and poor cooperation and excessive politics often mean that the leaks fall between the gaps in corporate responsibility.

The first problem is that people don't think across the revenue cycle. A product manager often won't concern himself with how a new service is billed—"That's for those back-office folks to take care of"—and a billing manager will rarely concern herself with the mysterious world of customer care representatives. At one large telecom company, in the early stages of planning a revenue maximization project, one network executive announced, rather innocently, "You know, we set up the switches to work, not to bill."

"In my opinion," the project director answered curtly, "if it doesn't bill, it doesn't work."

The second and more damaging effect of the silo mentality is that people fight across functions. In the healthcare industry, for instance, tensions between the patient-care side of an organization and the business side frequently stymie efforts to maximize revenue as the patient-care side sees back-office issues as unimportant and undeserving of resources compared to the life-and-death decisions made in hospital wards. (The business side, in return, is quick to remind the other side that bankrupt and shuttered hospitals do very little good for their patients.)

SUSCEPTIBILITIES: THE CULTURAL CAUSES

A telling time for us is always, in the early stages of a revenue maximization initiative, when we ask an assembled cross-functional group of executives to identify who is responsible for revenue maximization. Half the time, all the hands go up. Half the time, no hands go up.

Furthermore, in revenue maximization, as in life, people have a tendency to blame others for problems and show little concern for problems that they don't consider their own. One technology executive shared with us that during the first six months of a revenue maximization project she worked on, "The really tough challenge was to get buy-in from the operations side and from the sales side. Everyone thought that any billing errors were only related to our enterprise systems. Yet some of these errors were caused by service errors on the operations side and some were caused by contractual errors on the sales side." At a telecom company we worked with, a revenue maximization team ran thousands of test calls to test its network for regulatory and operational performance. The project identified problems worth millions of dollars in incremental revenue. The revenue maximization team would periodically run thousands of more test calls. And the test calls, periodically, would identify problems worth millions of dollars. The network function that could fix the network and capture the revenue never did anything because it hadn't bought into the project.

One final point: silos can occur geographically as well as functionally. (Sometimes both kinds can occur at the same time.) For example, one cable executive recently told our colleagues, "Right now, revenue assurance is viewed by the local markets as rearranging the deck chairs, just another corporate initiative that won't last."[3]

2. Cutting Muscle

Revenue maximization is difficult. It requires commitment and, above all, leadership. It also requires resources. When we discuss revenue maximization with companies unfamiliar with the concept, the first question is frequently a weary, "How much of our people's time will this take?" This question shouldn't be asked wearily. Capturing revenue leakage, also involves strengthening integrity.

One company we know of created a cross-functional revenue assurance committee designed to counteract the silo mentality. Yet the committee had no responsibility, no accountability, no CEO support, not a penny in resources, and not very much assigned employee time. It also had no attendance and produced no results. It was just another meeting. In the utilities industry, many companies find themselves without the technical expertise necessary to fight leakage because the skill sets required weren't necessary in the regulated era of fixed margins and returns.

A more serious problem than a static state of low resources is an active cutting of resources for revenue maximization. The biggest investment needed for the initiative is, for the most part, in people's time. But as our colleague noted about electric utilities, "Power companies are trying to operate as lean as possible. Since payroll and accounting are not viewed as profit centers, they usually see cuts, despite the fact that these offices are overwhelmed."[4] Similarly, one telecom executive, whose company is a customer of several large telecom companies, told us, "We've seen much more inaccuracies as organizations get slimmed down."

This cutting of revenue maximization muscle is happening in almost every industry and is happening for a variety of

SUSCEPTIBILITIES: THE CULTURAL CAUSES

reasons: control-oriented people being viewed as cost centers; an unawareness of the magnitude of revenue leakage; and the failure of revenue maximization professionals themselves to convince their companies of their potential to contribute to the bottom line.

In the telecom industry, a particularly disheartening trend has been that the people most likely to "take the package" of early retirement offered by cost-cutting companies are the senior middle managers who have decades of experience, who have a feel for their systems, who have an intuitive grasp of where the leaks are, and who often prevent greater leakage through undocumented, unofficial, but habitual actions. Telecom companies have also seen a decline in the skilled engineering and IT professionals necessary to complete revenue maximization projects.

3. COMPETITION FROM OTHER PRIORITIES

Peter Drucker once said that M&A activity is so popular not because of sound business reasoning but because it's a lot more fun than spending your day doing actual work.[5] Revenue maximization is, alas, actual work, and it is often viewed as a strategy only an accountant could love. "This isn't what's sexy," one executive told us. "This isn't what's fun. It's tough to mobilize the organization behind this because the organization likes fancy next-generation technology." And organizations like auditioning Hollywood starlets for major ad campaigns and negotiating intricate deals on the fourteenth tee.

One large telecom company, for example, spent a year implementing an automated tool—a billing accuracy project—that quantified millions in lost revenue. The tool examined three out of thousands of potential products for a month-long period and generated an ROI of nearly five to one. Yet with competing priorities sapping the company's will, the company essentially dropped the project and refused to make the *negligible* incremental investment to run the tool again in other areas and on other products. Assuming a similar error rate, the company could have achieved an ROI of 25 to 1 had it made the low investment necessary to expand the project.

Obviously, companies have other priorities, many with more sizzle and many offering greater financial opportunities than revenue maximization. (Before the recent economic slowdown, most companies had so many new initiatives that operations-focused initiatives like revenue maximization tended to get lost.) Clearly, executives have limited bandwidth and can concentrate on only so many initiatives, and frontline managers can only perform so many tasks in a day. Yet companies must understand that revenue leakage and potentially credibility-damaging revenue collection inaccuracies will occur unless confronting them is a high priority and unless profitability and integrity take precedence over "glitz and glam".

4. Defensiveness

Revenue leakage isn't always attributable to mistakes. But when it *is*, the blame game creates more problems than it solves. Sadly, executives and managers often react to revenue maximization initiatives by becoming defensive. Oftentimes, this happens when no one is blaming anyone. One member of our team, for example, performed a revenue maximization diagnostic for a business unit of a company and delivered his honest, agenda-free, blame-free view of revenue leakage and revenue growth opportunities. The company took the diagnostic as an attack and, essentially, refused to accept it.

We find the alter ego of defensiveness—excessive pride—to be prevalent at many companies. As one revenue maximization executive confided in us, in hushed tones, "There used to be an arrogance here that we're so good that we don't have problems" and thus no possibility of serious leakage. (They were wrong.) Excessive pride is a particular problem in the more technical areas of companies. Engineers and IT professionals are proud of their systems and equipment, often justifiably. Our billion-dollar, state-of-the-art systems, they claim, can't *possibly* leak. And they claim that an outside advisor can't possibly add value. Yet even new billion-dollar systems, in linking with other systems, or in how they are run, or in the quality of their inputs, allow the inaccurate, incomplete, or untimely collection of revenue to persist.

Defensiveness and pride sometimes produce comedy. At one telecom project we joined our client's revenue maximization team in identifying millions of dollars being lost through the faulty registering of data from the company's trunk groups. (A trunk group is a communication line between two switching systems in a telecom network.) Just as we began to quantify the leakage, trunk by trunk, so that we could form a plan to capture the leaked revenue, we found that, mysteriously, one of the trunks stopped leaking entirely. The network operations people had investigated and fixed the trunk without notifying anyone on the revenue maximization team. They did this, it turned out, two days after the problem was reported to them and after responding that the problem wasn't worth investigating at all.

5. The exceptions complex

Even in an age of frequent downsizing, almost every medium- or large-sized company has hundreds of people, often in football field-sized rooms, dedicated to manually auditing bills, reprocessing claims (in the healthcare industry), or handling exceptions—records "spit out" from systems because, for example, data is missing from certain fields. An "exceptions complex" often then arises around the mini-dukes and earls who have a vested interest in handling large volumes of exceptions and who are resistant to process improvements or automated tools to minimize them. "People are afraid of stopping exceptions," shared one executive we interviewed. "We have a huge company built on them. And if we go in and fix root cause of errors, it worries the director of some area dedicated to manually fixing exceptions. Because at our company, to be a director, everyone 'knows' that you have to have at least 100 people below you."

6. The control mindset

Integrating better controls into day-to-day processes is vital to revenue maximization, but a persistent control-orientation can hamper robust efforts to capture leakage. When a company measures success only by how many bills it audits or its regulatory compliance, it will rarely put forth the effort necessary to minimize leaks and maximize profitability and growth. Even more problematic, some companies claim to be "doing revenue assurance" when they are really only executing the basic, general ledger reconciliation and financial assurance controls done by every company.

7. A culture of extremes

Two "extreme" corporate cultures increase the susceptibility of revenue leakage: an aggressive culture of ready-fire-aim or an extraordinarily cautious culture.

A ready-fire-aim approach to major business decisions is hardly a new phenomenon, and, in many ways, it's praiseworthy. It helps companies avoid paralysis from too much analysis and planning. Yet, too often, fast-paced companies aren't doing the minimum necessary to prevent revenue leakage. "We are constantly changing our systems to meet competitive needs," one executive told us. "So we are always sprinting to keep up with the changes and to implement audits and processes to make sure that revenue streams are intact."

Ironically, aggressive, hot-footed companies with cultures of ready-fire-aim often become extremely cautious and prone to overplanning before launching a revenue maximization strategy made necessary, in part, by their agile corporate culture. They join other companies that are intractably, and frustratingly, too cautious, and that distrust revenue maximization as too new, too unproven, and too outside the company's comfort zone.

Proximate causes: technology, people, and processes

You can't catch a cold from being susceptible to one, no matter how often you go outside with your hair wet. In revenue leakage, too, susceptibilities only make a company more likely to leak. The *proximate* causes of direct and opportunity revenue leaks are flaws, misalignments, mistakes, omissions, and lapses related to people, processes, and technology, all of which undermine the integrity and availability of data. And as much as we would have liked to find more creative categories than this trusty old trio, the proximate causes of revenue leakage—and the corresponding strategies to address them—fit best into these categories.

Technology

The systems multiplying at most companies leak, sometimes almost inevitably, at their joints. Mainframes are not well connected to Web-based systems, data warehouses are not integrated into mainframe applications, financial systems are not fully linked to service-delivery systems, acquisitions' systems are not working with new patients' systems, and new product technologies are not seamlessly incorporated into legacy systems. Many hospitals, for instance, have 10 or more systems bolted onto their mainframe backbone managing the organization. New systems are added all the time. Alexander Cibenko of Saint Vincent Catholic Medical Centers of New York told us, "Systems interfaces are a huge issue. You have laboratory systems and radiology systems and cardiology systems and pharmacy systems that take in usage statistics, physician orders, and progress notes. They all generate transaction data that goes into an interface to generate billing. Without adequate design and testing, there is a large risk of leakage, and, even if the implementation is adequately planned, these interfaces require maintenance to continue to operate as designed. Many institutions do not have the daily controls and balancing procedures necessary to identify leakage that may happen on a regular or intermittent basis."

PROXIMATE CAUSES: TECHNOLOGY, PEOPLE AND PROCESSES

In the electric utilities industry too, as systems are added, leakage grows. As one of our colleagues said in a comment applicable to almost every industry, "The success factor of linking all these discrete systems together is not high. It is an enormously complicated task. There is a lot of lost data. And quite a bit of inefficiency in consolidation. It's fair to say that there probably isn't a single company, an energy supplier, that doesn't have some sort of billing problems, whether they realize it or not."[6]

Furthermore, systems weren't and aren't designed for an evolving marketplace. (At hospitals, for instance, according to Alexander Cibenko, "Governmental agencies, as well as numerous insurance companies, often develop new payment rules, or change existing payment rules, that we can't easily build into our current systems.") So, too in many projects, companies are choosing to spend resources on increasing functionality of the new systems rather than the integration, testing, and training necessary to ensure that the systems work. It is important to note that technology-caused leaks don't necessarily arise because the technology is broken. As Ann Sado, an Executive Vice President of Bell Canada, put it, "You can have a weak pipe because someone didn't screw it on tight enough or maybe because the coupling isn't designed properly. It's not necessarily a system problem."

So what, precisely, is going wrong because of faulty and inefficient connections between systems? Individual transaction records are being:

- Held in "suspense" by a system and purged, sometimes frequently, by that system because of insufficient record-holding capacity
- "Spit out" as exceptions requiring manual intervention, leading to delays and manual errors

- Deleted in connections between systems without any trace or explanation
- Inaccurately translated from one system to another.

In some cases, a *lack* of certain technology—or its economic unfeasibility—allows leaks to persist. In any initiative, eventually the money runs out, often before testing, and integration and training are completed, which are viewed as low priorities. We discuss some of the valuable preventive automated revenue maximization tools in Chapter 8.

People: we're only human

Eschelon's Rick Smith put it best: "Whenever you get into an environment rich with people manually entering things, sometimes multiple times, the only question you ought to ask yourself is, "How wrong is our data?" People cause revenue leakage by making mistakes, making qualitative assessments, and sometimes (and one hopes rarely) committing fraud, in other words, doing the things people do everyday.

Errors range from obvious sources of revenue leakage—a nurse forgetting to record that she administered an IV—to those with more complicated causes and effects. They include:

- **The classics.** People make mistakes. In the airline industry, for instance, agents who misprice tickets or fail to collect fees when an exchanged ticket costs more than an original ticket is a high-profile issue. Our colleagues estimate that errors in collecting exchange fees alone cost airlines 0.1 to 0.3 percent of total revenue.
- **Replicating errors.** In all industries, simple data entry errors—mistakes due to "fat fingers," as we call

them—can spawn major revenue inaccuracies damaging profitability or integrity when the errors are made in a master rate table. In one case, an electric utility invested millions of dollars to install a state-of-the-art automated meter that sent coded pulses, via telephone lines, to the utilities' headquarters to register real-time data for usage and billing purposes. Because the master rate table was wrong, however, the individual pulses were multiplied by the wrong amount by the billing system on the final customer invoices.

- **Interpretation errors.** Errors are sometimes less the fault of the error-maker than a function further upstream. In the telecom industry, for example, a marketing team will develop new products and hand off the billing requirements to the billing function. Often, however, the pricing of these products is so complicated or poorly documented that errors are inevitable. (If you sometimes can't decode the latest offer from a wireless service provider—the "Fun and Crazy" plan with discounts on full moons, even weekends, and Halloween, plus no roaming charges in Cincinnati, South Dakota, and Spain—you are not alone. The provider's billing department often can't decode it either.)

- **Plugging square pegs into round holes.** Also, in many industries, contracts for larger business customers have become extraordinarily complicated. They are frequently more a matter of art than science. Thus, for example, when a telecom salesperson is asked to quote a price on a dedicated frame relay link between New Hampshire and Sweden, he or she, more interested in getting the sale, will often quote a price—with creativity and a fair amount of fudge factoring—and let the billing for the service "work itself out." Similarly, customer service representatives often do not have the time or patience to work with new edits in IT systems and find ways to work around them. For example, they will not complete all the steps of a credit check procedure, or if a system allows an automatic $25 credit to a complaining customer and not a $50 credit, a representative will give two $25 credits just to appease the customer and get on with her day.

- **Rushed provisioning.** One telecom executive we spoke to lamented that human errors are sometimes unavoidable because customers place unreasonable demands on companies to set up services quickly. If, as she said, a customer gives 48 hours notice to install phone service for an entire building—not as unusual a request as it may seem—some lines, inevitably, won't be correctly provisioned or billed, and some assets will be lost.

We'll mercifully end this cataloguing of the frailties of the human species here. Yet one more point must be made: *manual begets manual.* If a person in one function makes a mistake, it often necessitates manual reworking and thus the opportunity for a colleague in another function to make another mistake. For instance, when two systems require a manual file transfer and "swivel chair automation," as Susan McNeice of telecom industry publisher TeleStrategies calls it, there is a higher likelihood of error, exceptions, and manual reworking. A good portion of the claims re-work effort at healthcare companies has its root cause in manual errors made during original capture of charges or patient information.

Qualitative assessments. Defensible, logical, explicable human judgment can also cause revenue leakage. In many companies, uncoordinated, independent decisions that may make sense in isolation can add up to major sources of revenue leakage if not properly controlled. The primary cause of judgment-related errors is what is known as "adjustments" in the telecom industry: salespeople and customer care representatives giving squeaky wheels the grease. Often, the amount of grease is left to a customer-service representative or salesperson's discretion.

The squeak of customer complaints can become particularly deafening when there are problems in the underlying service. For cable, telecom, and Internet companies, launching of new technology-related services has frequently prefaced unhealthy levels of adjustments. "Whenever you get into new product offerings," a cable executive explained, "you run a higher risk of technical failure or customer dissatisfaction. And you end up with customer service reps cutting deals that perhaps they shouldn't."[7]

Finally, both internal and external fraud is a major source of revenue leakage. In some industry sectors, such as DBS operators and some electric utilities, combating fraud is the primary—or only—focus of revenue maximization-like activities. (Some executives in these industries, by the way, see fraud exclusively as a cost issue, not as a cause of revenue leakage.)

Processes

In many of the above cases—especially in situations when manual work begets more manual work—the propensity for error is not a function of the individual, but the process. In this book, especially in Chapter 7, we talk a lot about integrating revenue maximization into day-to-day processes. The reason is simple: revenue leakage often occurs because processes are unformed, complicated, flawed, or considered unimportant.

In many cases, companies don't have any processes or business rules where they're needed. For instance, one company we worked with awarded salespeople a commission for every order signed up. Frequently, however, customers canceled the original order. The company had no process in place to determine what percentage of the commission the salesperson was entitled to keep if the services were canceled.

Other processes are just too complicated. The healthcare industry is, in the words of a colleague, "code crazy." Even though healthcare organizations employ teams of certified medical record coders, the number of tables and profiles and claim-form logic can still be mind-boggling when coders enter individual patient episodes and procedures and "abstract" this information into an organization's systems.

Other times, employees appear not to know about certain processes. At one telecom company we worked with, a series of switches was not recording data needed for billing purposes. We and the revenue maximization team originally thought that the technology had malfunctioned. In fact, the switches were working properly, and they were eventually reprogrammed. What was causing the leaks? The people responsible for originally setting up the switches had not followed (or not known about) the billing verification processes needed.

In this case, a proximate cause (a poorly designed process) was probably aggravated by cultural susceptibilities—maybe a culture of ready-fire-aim, maybe a low

PROXIMATE CAUSES: TECHNOLOGY, PEOPLE AND PROCESSES

priority given to control-oriented revenue maximization steps like process verification—which, at the bottom, were caused by temporal causes: the rush to sell a new type of product in a field opened up by deregulation. So, too, beneath almost every penny of revenue leakage lies deep and overlapping cultural and technical causes. That is why stopping the leaks—maximizing revenue, improving profitability, integrity, and growth—requires equally deep and overlapping cultural and technical strategies, all vigorously pursued.

NOTES

1. Darren Henderson and Rosie Lombardi, "Are Your Systems Leaking Revenue?," *CIO Canada*, 1 June 2000.

2. Mary Chris Jaklevic, "Revenue Stopper: Bungled Billing System Conversions Are Plaguing the Hospital Industry," *Modern Healthcare*, 2 July 2001, 36.

3. PricewaterhouseCoopers, "Broadband on the Brink: The Growing Importance of Revenue Assurance in the Cable and DBS Industry" (New York: PricewaterhouseCoopers, May 2002), 7.

4. Ed Tobia, quoted in PricewaterhouseCoopers, "About That Revenue Leakage," *Power Executive* (New York: PricewaterhouseCoopers, 2 June 2001), 2.

5. Jim Collins, *From Good to Great* (New York: Harper Collins, 2001), 180.

6. Michael Hurle, quoted in PricewaterhouseCoopers, "About that Revenue Leakage," 1.

7. PricewaterhouseCoopers, "Broadband on the Brink," 3.

CHAPTER FOUR

WHAT COMPANIES ARE DOING NOW

Rick Smith, President of telecom company Eschelon, candidly admitted to us that he was once a dismisser of revenue maximization. "I think I was part of the problem," he said. "When you first hear someone questioning your data, your first response is to so say, Wrong. Our stuff is good. We don't have problems." Rick, of course, changed. "You have to get over that real quickly. You have to get into projects, thinking, The data is wrong. Now let's find out how wrong it is."

Most companies have shared the first response of Rick and Eschelon. Only a few leading companies have experienced Eschelon's change in attitude.

Before exploring the details of revenue maximization strategies that will allow companies to grow earnings and bolster corporate integrity, we want to examine what companies are doing now and what have they done in the past.

This chapter provides a brief history of revenue maximization and a bird's-eye survey of the general path of commitment to revenue maximization that has taken companies from resistance to enthusiasm, or in most cases, to a step in between. In doing so, we hope to situate revenue maximization as a real-world strategy pursued (or not) by real companies in a real historical context, and not a speculative strategy dreamed up, among the beakers in a lab.

A VERY SHORT HISTORY OF REVENUE MAXIMIZATION

Evolutionary biologists talk about a process of "speciation" in which small evolutionary changes eventually create new, distinct species. Compared to a program like Six Sigma, which was created almost full-blown by a group of Motorola quality control executives, the speciation of revenue maximization has been a subtler process.

Decades of projects and initiatives fill the revenue maximization family tree. Companies have long launched, in pockets, initiatives to combat revenue leakage, especially in the credits and collections areas. So too, any time companies improved the accuracy of a system or reconciled a sub-ledger to a general ledger or focused on revenue collection in a profit- or operating-improvement initiative, they pursued partial forms of what we call revenue maximization. Many of these early programs were (and are) forceful, such as many companies' robust anti-fraud programs and comprehensive IT strategies to replace manual processes with automated solutions. Yet companies, at least in the industries discussed in this book, performed most of these projects from a control perspective—solving a problem, not seizing an opportu-

A SHORT HISTORY OF REVENUE MAXIMIZATION 73

nity for revenue growth, for increased profitability, and for greater integrity. Moreover, except for the occasional enterprisewide systems upgrade, most of these programs were buried in the proverbial (and sometimes actual) boondocks of a company. Revenue maximization-like jobs were low paying. They were viewed as low value to the organization. Companies, for instance, located their billing validation centers, crammed with rooms of bill checkers, in the lowest-cost area, far from the buzz of corporate headquarters and far from the more glamorous strategic and M&A work.

THE TELECOM INDUSTRY FOCUSES ON LEAKAGE

Over the last five years, though, revenue assurance has risen in importance in many industries as the magnitude of leakage has increased. The telecom industry, for example, has had a robust recent history of revenue maximization because it has had a robust recent history of revenue leakage. In just ten years, the industry faced the end of guaranteed rates of return (1992), the opening up of competition to a whole new class of companies (1996), and head-spinning experiences with every single temporal cause of revenue leakage: new products, new technologies, new competitive landscapes, and frequent mergers and acquisitions. Understandably, all this increased revenue leakage and revenue collection inaccuracies industry-wide, although executives had little time to worry about it. That is, until the last two years. Today, the global telecom industry is undergoing what L. William Seidman, Chairman of the FDIC during the 1980s savings and loan crisis, called, "the largest single meltdown in a defined industry I've ever seen."[1] Every company now struggles to achieve basic profitability; 63 U.S. telecom companies have announced bankruptcy in the last two years; and perhaps as much as half of $880 *billion* in debt, equity, and bank loans raised by the U.S. industry since 1997 has been lost.[2] Even the total number of local phone lines in the United States has shrunk to 179.8 million in 2001 from 188.6 million in 2000, the first annual decline recorded since the 1984 breakup of AT&T.[3]

During (and due) to this wrenching roller coaster ride, revenue maximization as a growth and profitability strategy was born with a new intensity and attitude, as a new species in the telecom industry. Companies have bought and applied revenue maximization technology. Others have created formal functions that are now held accountable to add incremental revenue. Many companies—and this innovation shouldn't be underestimated—are pursuing revenue maximization projects with quantified goals and ROIs. Before, few particularly cared to prove the value proposition of revenue maximization activities.

We don't want to overstate the achievements. In August 2001, we wrote a white paper that studied the state of revenue maximization in the telecom industry and gave the industry an overall C+ on its "report card." The grade has improved only slightly since then. But, as Susan McNeice of TeleStrategies reminded us, the telecom industry has made impressive progress. It has gone through three phases of revenue assurance in the last three years, from addressing only specific problems—primarily intercarrier relationships—to realizing that revenue maximization was a whole company issue, to realizing that it may be, in her words, a "survivability issue."

A SHORT HISTORY OF REVENUE MAXIMIZATION 75

THE SPECIATION POINT

If there was a single point of speciation in the telecom industry, when a growling wolf became a lovable dog, it was the 1998 TeleStrategies conference dedicated to revenue assurance. There, we heard for the first time of broader industry interest in something called revenue assurance. According to Jeff Sklaver, who conceived of the conference, TeleStrategies had scheduled it after receiving two proposals for revenue assurance panels at a larger industry conference. The first conference was, as they say about some weddings, an understated affair, with only 50 attendees and a lonely folding table promoting a lonely automated tool.

Five times the number of people attended the same conference in 2001. There are now two conferences a year. At these events, participants encounter a full trade show with booth after booth of specialty technology companies, billing providers, and all the major strategic advisory and technology firms pitching revenue assurance tools and handing out key chains. (There, we teach a "master class" in revenue maximization targeted to the large part of the audience that has moved beyond the need for basic information on the outlines of the strategy.) Nowadays, in the telecom industry, most people know about revenue assurance, and everyone recognizes it as an issue. And if there are still miles of road to be marched, revenue maximization functions are steadily achieving more corporate support and quantified success.

Our personal history with revenue maximization has paralleled the industry's. In the late 1990s, we were working in the telecom industry and had experience conducting the occasional revenue assurance project. Early in 1998, we and our colleague, Luke Sayers, recognized that capturing revenue leakage and stopping inaccuracies represented a major growth opportunity within almost all telecom companies. However, most companies had yet to grasp the tactics and strategies needed to actually capture revenue. Few doors opened for us at first. Those that did belonged to lower level managers. While we anticipated skepticism, we didn't expect the occasional hostility—the "We've been working on our systems forever. What, Mr. Advisor, can you possibly add?" Yet, because of the growing interest in revenue leakage and the success achieved by early adopters, our telecom team has grown to 300 dedicated professionals working on revenue maximization projects around the world. Many of our colleagues at PricewaterhouseCoopers working with other industries have experienced similar growth in interest and scale.

A full history of revenue maximization, which would be of phenomenally little interest to anyone, would be a story of uncoordinated speciation, with industries arriving at greater commitment independently. The healthcare industry, for example, started seriously focusing on revenue cycle enhancement around 1996 as managed care arrangements (like HMOs and PPOs) proliferated and new payment methodologies (like case rates and full or partial capitation) spread. The cable, utility, and technology services industries have had very short histories of revenue maximization: most companies in those industries are only starting to focus on the issues now.

THE PATH TO COMMITMENT

When we considered methodically what companies are doing now in revenue maximization and reviewed the experiences of companies we've worked with or observed, we discovered a pattern—a general path of commitment to revenue maximization. While the path we describe may be a bit too tidy, we think it describes empirically what has happened—and what is happening—at many companies. In our experience, companies on the path to revenue maximization commitment go through five phases: the resistant, the dabblers, the stalled, the dedicated, and the enthusiasts. Not every company goes through every phase, and, in many large companies, a hodgepodge of business units are in different phases simultaneously. Yet, every company can be classified into one of these phases, as Figure 4.1 illustrates.

Figure 4.1
Path to Commitment

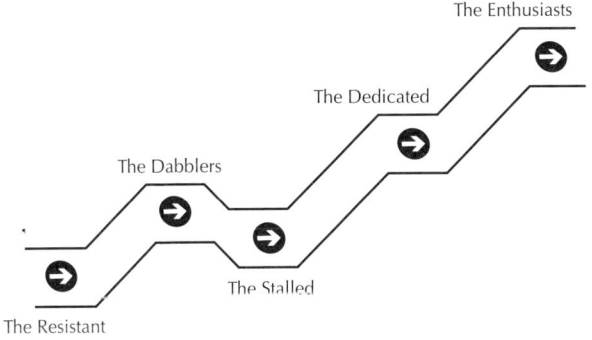

1. THE RESISTANT

Never in the course of human events has a company decided to pursue a vigorous revenue maximization strategy when first presented with the business case to do so. There is *always* a period of resistance, a period marked by a confluence of attitudes opposing action. Oftentimes, two executives within a company will agree not to take action but strongly disagree on the reason for their decision. There are four primary variants of resistance:

The unaware. Sometimes, companies or executives have never heard of revenue assurance (and certainly never of revenue maximization). Sometimes, their eyes fill with a far-off look of dim recognition, as if trying to remember the historical importance of the Proclamation of 1763. Just as often, 17 executives at a single company operate under 17 different definitions of revenue assurance. (Gartner Dataquest notes that because many strategic advisors and tool vendors use the term revenue assurance indiscriminately, the term has become "something like a meaningless placeholder." And "often, telecom executives are at a loss about the real meaning and value of revenue assurance."[4]) Our team surveyed cable and DBS executives on revenue maximization in the summer of 2002. As expected, we found that almost 40 percent of executives couldn't estimate margin leakage at their companies. Yet, equally interesting, we found that individuals within companies had radically different notions of what "revenue assurance" was and what their own companies were doing about the strategy.[5] A colleague reflected on broadband executives' recent attitudes: "They didn't really know what we meant when we talked about revenue assurance. They thought it was just cash reconciliation, which is really a basic control technique that every company does." This, in the broadband industry, has begun to change.

The dismissers. Some resistant executives are not shy about their opinions. Revenue maximization, they insist, is not a worthwhile initiative. As one cable executive said, margin leakage "will work itself out over time…I don't think it's material in any way."[6] Some dismissers are more immovable in their opinion that revenue maximization is snake-oil advisor-speak.

At some companies, the aggressive dismissal arose, in our opinion, because the companies had no sense of how much they actually leak or the financial opportunities available within the companies. The Catch-22 is that they can't have a sense of the opportunity available from an investment in revenue maximization because getting that sense requires some investment to diagnose and quantify leakage.

The self-congratulators I. Companies and executives periodically go through periods of revenue maximization self-congratulation. Resistant executives argue that they are already tackling revenue maximization completely and robustly. As utilities executives occasionally (and mistakenly) tell our colleagues, "We already have a project doing this, and we know more about this than you." Sometimes, specific areas warrant self-congratulation: many companies resistant to revenue maximization have done good jobs in isolated areas, for example, in combating fraud or reducing the aging of receivables. Many companies are also right to congratulate themselves on vigilant internal audit functions and disciplined control environments.

However, when this self-congratulation comes atop an excuse not to pursue revenue maximization more thoroughly, it is frequently based on an extremely narrow definition of revenue maximization. Revenue maximization, in this view, is a strategy to handle only narrow problems. In the telecom industry, for instance, the strategy is first seen, in Qwest's Pat Walker's words, "as all about billing and getting billing correct." And companies with a billing auditing program then believe that they have "done" revenue maximization, end of story.

The tolerators. Some executives and companies resistant to revenue maximization aren't resistant to the concept of revenue leakage. They accept that leakage and inaccurate revenue collection is a problem—or an irritant—but believe that they are a cost of doing business or that their companies can't do anything about them. We have long called this attitude the "mental write-off." It often drips from a general sense of fatalism. One revenue maximization executive described for us the fatalism at her company: "People in all departments say, essentially, there is no way to expect people to do accurate transactions. The mindset is that we'll always have errors." We have spoken time and again with executives who admit to identifying major revenue maximization opportunities—often $2 or $3 million from a few small projects—but who show little interest in actually launching a project to capture them, unable to imagine that 50 such initiatives may exist, with a large aggregate impact.

Some executives demonstrate a sincere hope that the company will get around to addressing revenue leakage more thoroughly someday, but someday always turns out to be next quarter.

Finally, some tolerators have a very good excuse to accept revenue leakage: they are in a regulated industry. Many gas, water, and electric utilities around the world face no pressure to minimize leakage as it is, literally, considered a cost of doing business, and is added to a company's rate base, and recovered in higher prices.

2. THE DABBLERS

Most companies eventually accept the importance of revenue maximization, but, rarely in our experience, does this acceptance immediately lead to a formal, energetic program. Companies seem to slip gradually into a program rather than seize the opportunity, eyes-open, with both hands.

The dabbler phase, as we call it, carries an implicit recognition that revenue maximization should be pursued. But a pokiness in pursuing it reveals a lack of real conviction. Often, senior executives will politely smile at internal champions of the initiative and forget about them when they walk out the door. Frequently, a company will form a committee or assign a person to study the issues. A few telecom companies, for instance, are diligent about sending employees to conferences even if the employees never seem to have accomplished anything in the 364 days between gatherings.

Other than the general cultural susceptibilities, there are four main reasons why companies dabble:

- Most commonly, the value of revenue maximization has not yet been fully verified by widespread experience and success.

- Often, companies concentrate their resources on developing an elegant "giant leap" solution to revenue leakage that will supposedly pay off big a few years down the road.

- Other companies presume that revenue maximization must be a giant leap and file it in a "too hard" or a "too big" basket.

- Many companies suffer from an old-fashioned, all-too-human fear of failure.

What dabblers do. The dabbler phase is like a garden. Companies plant a few programs here and there—an automated tool, a reengineered process, a few people allocated to a task—rather than create a productive, profit-generating, revenue-maximizing, integrity-improving farm. In this phase, revenue maximization projects tend to be reactive or sometimes mere Band-Aid responses. A certain *voluntary* feel pervades the whole effort. An executive we spoke to sighed as she described the "revenue assurance team" attached to the CFO's office in each business unit of her company. It is really, she told us, nothing more than "a gopher group," tackling the smallest of problems and rarely accomplishing anything.

The dabbler phase, though oftentimes frustrating for revenue maximization zealots in dabbling companies, is not necessarily bad. In many cases, dabbling creates the initial successes necessary for a revenue maximization strategy to snowball and achieve more and greater success. Dabbling is often an *advisable* way for a company to begin a program and avoid the dangers of trying, as we say, to boil the whole ocean.

3. THE STALLED

We have heard a rumor that, at some companies, commitment to revenue maximization moves smoothly and naturally upward from the dabbler phase to a phase of true dedication. We have never been so fortunate to see this happen ourselves. In our experience, companies always stall—or take a step backward—on the path to commitment. Sometimes, stalling arises as a by-product of unrelated factors, as when a company, for instance, moves people spearheading revenue maximization to other tasks or faces competing priorities or cost-cutting pressures. One healthcare executive told us that because of a "revenue cycle" project, "We collected $50 million more than we otherwise would have. At the same time, when you can't buy a CAT

COMMITMENT PHASES: THE DABBLERS

scan, all of a sudden it becomes an issue and people ask why do you need consultants and why is there this so-called opportunity in the first place."

More often, though, companies stall because of dissatisfaction with early revenue maximization initiatives or over-satisfaction with them.

The grumblers. Many companies we have worked with or observed have gone through a post-dabbling—or inter-dabbling—phase of grumbling about revenue maximization. In some cases, executives were disappointed by the results of a project because a few projects suffered from "the melt factor," in which captured revenue was less than originally quantified or more difficult to capture than expected. In some cases, a vendor oversold the benefits. (Every strategic and technical advisor, including us, is sometimes too optimistic.) In other cases, when a project turned out not to be the silver bullet—a silver bullet that rarely, if ever, exists in revenue maximization—enthusiasm for the whole strategy waned. And in some cases, the grumbling arose from a self-defeating cycle. The longer a company dawdled and dabbled, the more resources it frittered away, and more it lowered the ROI of a completed initiative.

The self-congratulators II. Most revenue maximization projects do meet expectations. However, instead of initial success feeding into a greater appetite for deeper and more challenging revenue maximization activities, as we once expected would always happen, some companies pat themselves on the stomach after a dabbler phase, reach for a toothpick, and announce triumphantly that they have "done revenue assurance."

When we work with a company through a brainstorming or formal diagnostic, the process will often reveal dozens (sometimes hundreds) of revenue maximization projects that are worthwhile to pursue. The company, by necessity, will narrow these hundreds to a starting point, usually five or so initial projects. Yet when the company completes the five *starting point* projects, an amnesia frequently sets in. The company will announce that it has the problem licked, completely forgetting about the dozens of projects arising from the original diagnostic.

Sometimes, self-congratulators border on the self-delusional. Our colleagues, for example, encountered one electric utility that boasted of nearly 100 different revenue-related projects. Yet when they assessed the projects, none were maximizing revenue or achieving any measurable results, and more than half weren't real projects at all.

4. The dedicated

Some companies are doing the right things. They are pursuing revenue maximization on all four strategic fronts. They are *proactively* and, dynamically implementing technology tools, changing processes, creating organizational change, and establishing monitoring mechanisms. They are boosting growth, profits, and integrity. These companies moved through self-congratulation and grumbling with a clearer idea of the realistic—and still very attractive—opportunities in revenue maximization. They also have a clearer idea, as Terry Mosey, President of Bell Ontario, told us, that revenue maximization "is a journey"—with challenges, lessons, occasional steps backwards, and occasional wrong turns.

Being a dedicated company does not require that the entire organization—every executive, every board member—is dedicated to revenue maximization. It only requires that *enough* people, champions, are dedicated to the strategy to ensure that a company is actively maximizing revenue in the areas that these champions control.

The oft-cited Bell Canada is the prime example of a dedicated company. As we said in Chapter 1, the company captured C$67 million in its full year of effort. It is also the first large-cap telecom company we know of to have undergone a formal organizational analysis to determine the ideal allocation of resources between individual business units' revenue maximization teams and its corporate revenue maximization function.

Revenue maximization champions at Bell Canada unashamedly admit they can do more. They expend considerable energy and executive clout "infiltrating," as they say, Bell Canada at large. They are trying to generate more enterprisewide commitment, more resources for revenue maximization, and more robust programs in other business units. They are trying to move Bell Canada to the enthusiast phase.

5. The Enthusiasts

When Bill Bradley ran for the U.S. Presidency in 2000, he talked about racial reconciliation as *his* issue for "pleasing the boss." Citing Ronald Reagan's "please the boss" issue of cutting taxes, Bradley explained that more important than proposing specific programs was creating an environment in his hoped-for administration in which everyone knew that the way to please the boss was to work for racial reconciliation. The situation is much the same at revenue maximization companies that have reached the enthusiast level, the highest level on the path of commitment. At these companies, the key driver is strong leadership: CEOs and other high-profile executives make it clear to the entire organization that maximizing revenue and making revenue collection timely, accurate, and complete are top corporate priorities. Executives and frontline managers, on their own, strive to find new and aggressive ways to maximize revenue. They strive to please the boss.

Like a dedicated company, an enthusiast company dynamically and comprehensively pursues all four best-practice revenue maximization strategies, but enthusiasts' efforts are much broader and encounter much less intracorporate resistance. Enthusiast companies may be doing 50 revenue maximization projects a year, 30 of them repeatable, 20 one-time in nature. Their leadership creates passion and intensity for revenue maximization. (It is often one of the top four or five priorities of a CEO's career.) Eventually, integrating new revenue maximization processes and considering the potential revenue leakage impact of *all* corporate action becomes, as Terry Mosey phrased it, "as natural as getting a cup of coffee in the morning."

A few healthcare companies have become enthusiasts. According to our colleagues, a survey of large healthcare systems recently ranked revenue cycle management as the chief concern of the systems' CEOs. And the executives dedicated to revenue maximization at healthcare companies have increased their profiles (and their salaries) remarkably in the last five years.

The irony: looping the loop. The irony of the path to commitment is that truly enthusiastic companies, after the first few years of their enthusiasm, probably have less opportunity for incremental earnings growth from revenue maximization than dabbler companies do. The law of diminishing returns can apply fiercely to revenue maximization. Enthusiastic maximizers simply leak less. It is easy then to imagine how the passion and intensity for the initiative could diminish and how an aggressive growth and profitability improvement focus could slide back into a more passive control orientation. In other words, it's easy to see how revenue maximization could turn full circle.

For example, from a distance, the financial services industry appears to share many of the characteristics of resistant companies. Companies in this industry have little awareness of formal growth strategies like revenue cycle enhancement or revenue maximization. Most financial services companies congratulate themselves on their rigor in launching relatively narrow solutions to tackle narrow potential leakage problems, such as assuring proper payments in credit card affinity programs. And all of their activities have a notable control orientation, partly due to the strict regulatory oversight of banks throughout the world, partly due to the particularly high concern about overbilling of fees because of vigilant consumer advocacy groups, and partly due to the directness and relative ease of tracking services and payments in dollars or other currency (and thus forgoing the processes and technology needed to convert services into monetary values).

At the same time, many companies in the financial services industry match the characteristics of revenue maximization enthusiasts, even if they don't know the term. The companies do not go to market if they cannot bill for a service; they rigorously test new systems and product launches; they are very good at preventing revenue collection inaccuracies following mergers and acquisitions. In short, they are intolerant of leakage.

Our colleagues note that the focus on revenue leakage comes in peaks and valleys in the financial services industry, and every few years a company gets made an example of, thus reenergizing industry vigilance. Whether or not the industry's rigorous control-orientation—its "post-enthusiast" phase—is sustainable in the long term is difficult to answer. Frankly, the question is not particularly relevant for most companies in other sectors. Any worry about the ability to sustain an aggressive revenue maximization culture in the face of diminishing revenue leakage is worry that most companies should be lucky to have.

And every company, nowadays, must pursue robust revenue maximization activities to strengthen corporate integrity, improve the accuracy of its bills and financial statements, and protect its corporate reputation regardless of the earnings growth potential from these activities.

Moving up the path to commitment

Companies don't amble nonchalantly up the revenue maximization path to commitment. Forces compel them upwards. The four main motive forces are:

- Earnings pressure
- Outside peer pressure
- Internal peer pressure
- Intrinsic motivation

Almost all companies feel *all* of the forces at some time in their revenue maximization experience.

Earnings pressure. Rare is the company that does not feel earnings pressure at every moment of the day, but it is hardly a coincidence that the healthcare industry, for example, began concentrating on revenue maximization when managed care contracts started mercilessly pressuring margins, or that telecom and cable companies have begun focusing—or focusing more seriously—on revenue maximization now, when both industries face severe and unprecedented challenges to profitability. One telecom company, for instance, began to focus on revenue leakage only after discovering and correcting, in the words of one of its executives, "a huge underbilling problem that had been going on for years and years." Earnings pressure—and the accompanying focus on leakage—is often felt at an individual level. "When times got tough in the telecom industry," one executive told us, "people's own personal finances seemed at stake, and they started concentrating again on the bread-and-butter aspects of the business. They said, Hold on a minute. We can't afford to give away stuff anymore." Another company admitted to us that its embrace of revenue maximization arose directly from aggressive growth objectives, few growth opportunities in its core business, and severe capital expenditure limits.

Sometimes, the earnings pressure that drives forward revenue maximization commitment is acute. AT&T, for example, built its revenue assurance management process five years ago, after experiencing what Tom Berry called "a cold shower" due to a specific credit and collection issue. At other companies, rash operating decisions taken to accelerate earnings growth led companies to do the wrong thing and exacerbate the proximate causes of revenue leakage.

While AT&T and others leveraged their focus on specific issues into broader revenue maximization programs, the crises at other companies have unfortunately not produced lasting change. For example, we worked on a project three years ago with a telecom company after it experienced a sudden revenue dip. Company executives hypothesized that the dip was caused by its billing system, and we investigated potential leaks. We focused our analysis on one product for one month in one of several billing systems. That billing system, we found, did not leak. The revenue dip was due to other issues. (Customers, as it were, were marching pretty steadily out the door.) The executives took this "good news," however, as validation that they did not need a revenue maximization program at all, and ended the project, as they began, as dismissers of revenue maximization.

Outside peer pressure. In industries where many companies are now pursuing revenue maximization-like activities, outside peer pressure—trade journals, revenue assurance conferences, informal dialogues—has frequently driven individual companies up the path of commitment. The peer pressure mechanisms in the healthcare industry are particularly robust. Trade groups like the Healthcare Financial Management Association have created credentialing programs in revenue cycle management. The association also sponsors initiatives like the "patient-friendly billing project" to spread best practices.

Internal peer pressure. At large companies, internal peer pressure can drive greater enterprisewide commitment to revenue maximization. For example, when Terry Mosey sits on the executive council of Bell Canada and shares the revenue maximization successes at Bell Ontario, he motivates other business units to explore the opportunities of the strategy. Similarly, our colleagues have noticed that, in the decentralized cable industry, if a revenue maximization project is really successful in one market, the other markets "beg to get in."

Intrinsic motivation. In *In Search of Excellence,* Tom Peters and Robert Waterman wrote about how excellent companies seize upon an intrinsic motivation to achieve greater success.[7] So too in revenue maximization. As Karin Wagar of Verizon told us, "The hardest thing to do was getting through the first hurdles, but the momentum since then has been unbelievable." Whether we think of a company's rapidly blooming intrinsic motivation as a function of achieving critical mass, reaching a tipping point, or turning a flywheel, the results are the same: people become excited about maximizing revenue, success breeds more success, and action impels more and accelerated action. Executives are leading the troops and troops are pushing executives all in the same direction. Occasionally, the actual tipping point is outside—earnings or peer—pressure, and occasionally, executives one day just seem to "get it" and understand the opportunities within their companies. Whatever the trigger, this intrinsic motivation becomes the prime engine of dedicated and enthusiastic companies.

Industry paths follow industry dynamics

Detailing the variations of the path to commitment in every industry would be an academic exercise of dubious value. However, two generalizations are worth making:

- A slow move up the path of commitment generally occurs in industries with bigger, more inertial enterprises like the major telecom companies; industries with smaller and more flexible organizations move up the path more quickly.

- Industries with a multitude of players and diverse competitive dynamics, such as the utilities industry, tend to move more slowly up the path than concentrated industries with more common competitive dynamics like cable operators.

Whatever the generalizations, no company will move up the path to commitment, slowly or quickly, smoothly or sputteringly, unless it successfully maximizes revenue and captures real value.

How precisely to do that is the focus of the rest of this book.

Notes

1. Peter S. Goodman, "Telecom Sector May Find Past Is Its Future," *Washington Post*, 8 July 2002, A01.

2. Estimate of Richard J. Peterson, Chief Market Strategist of Thomson Financial, quoted in Goodman, "Telecom Sector."

3. Seth Schiesel with Simon Romero, "Regional Bell Giants No Longer Invulnerable," *The New York Times*, 23 July 2002, C6.

4. Scholz, "Revenue Assurance Services Providers," 1.

5. PricewaterhouseCoopers, "Broadband on the Brink," 2.

6. PricewaterhouseCoopers, "Broadband on the Brink," 2.

7. Thomas J. Peters and Robert H. Waterman, Jr., *In Search of Excellence: Lessons from America's Best-Run Companies* (New York Warner Books, 1982), 72.

CHAPTER FIVE

KEYS TO SUCCESS: MANAGING A REVENUE MAXIMIZATION INITIATIVE

We've made our case for the strengthening of growth, profitability, and integrity through revenue maximization, for the pervasiveness and seriousness of revenue leakage, and for the still underdeveloped responses to the issues by many companies. A company not convinced that it should at least more actively consider revenue maximization must, in that case, ask itself candidly *why* it is different from the hundreds of other companies who, at one point, also thought themselves immune from the incomplete, inaccurate, or untimely collection of revenue.

From here on, starting with six keys to success, we focus exclusively on what companies should do to maximize revenue.

The strategies repeated. For those still in the shadows of the gloom of the problem, we remind them of the way out: the four core strategies of integrating revenue maximization into day-to-day processes, implementing key automated tools, creating a revenue-responsible organization, and surrounding all these with quantifiable monitoring mechanisms. And, again, we advise implementing these strategies through the recipe steps of identify, quantify, capture. The most gratifying recipe step, obviously, is capture, and, as we discuss the benefits of each strategy in Chapters 7 through 10, it is vital to remember that these strategies exist for two main purposes: first, to strengthen corporate integrity; second and, more centrally, to capture more revenue. This capture comes in four flavors:

- **Immediate capture,** the most obvious form, in which a company corrects inaccurate or incomplete transaction data and either back bills for services already provided or begins to bill correctly for recurring services
- **Preventive capture,** perhaps the most important form, in which a company proactively addresses root causes of revenue leakage and prevents leaks from happening in the first place
- **Opportunity capture,** in which a company addresses and corrects processes or systems that are blocking incremental revenue
- **Efficiency capture,** in which a company achieves operating efficiencies in revenue maximization-related activities

The tactical and strategic actions we advise over the next few chapters may seem intimidating, overwhelming, and as we've been accused of being once or twice, a touch fanatical. Yet we are laying out an ideal, a *best-practice* revenue maximization strategy. Companies trying to seize the financial opportunities must understand the depth of commitment required to fully maximize revenue.

However, to return to the kitchen for our metaphors, revenue maximization is not a soufflé in which a cook either delivers a big, impressive success or a droopy, collapsed failure. Yes, capturing revenue growth of 2 to 5 percent (a range that can be higher or lower depending on the industry) requires, in our opinion, a company to do *all four* strategies thoroughly and energetically. Yet a company can still achieve sizable and high-return benefits if it only does one or two strategies, or all of the strategies in only one business unit, or some of the strategies with very little pep or zip. This, we believe, makes revenue maximization a "no-brainer" for most companies. Forget for a moment about NPV calculations. Forget about the five-year budget. Even small actions in this initiative can generate payback within 90 days.

For the big payback, however, companies must remember that *revenue maximization is a multi-year strategy*. It takes time for a company to weave it into its business as an integral, critical part of its core mission. But *revenue maximization gets easier*. All of the following strategies and success factors that today may seem overly demanding or mere wishful-thinking can become old-hat once a revenue maximization program is up and running. "You get a feel for it," Mike McGrath explained. "You get in the zone, and you're really able to prioritize. Some projects you just know are slam dunks. And you know that you can do them in three weeks."

The six keys. The keys to success that follow are directed at the champions, the replicators, the evangelists, the early adopters, and all the other people (described by all the other cyber-management buzzwords) who take it upon themselves to lead the charge against inaccurate and incomplete revenue collection. These keys to success are about managing a revenue maximization initiative, and they are no less essential than the four core strategies or individual project tactics. To achieve success, revenue maximization champions should, as Figure 5.1 illustrates:

1. **Act holistically.** Address issues across functions, link all core strategies, and integrate revenue maximization into broader business decisions.
2. **See the forest and the trees.** Combine a strategic vision and a tactical focus on the operating details.
3. **Speak in dollars and cents.** Make the initiative concrete.
4. **Be relentless.** When facing roadblocks, knock them over or go around them.
5. **Do something.** Have a bias for action.
6. **Manage success.** Grow the strategy's scope and build support for it by actively managing success.

Figure 5.1
Six Keys to Success

Anyone familiar with management books—or, frankly, human experience—will recognize that some of these keys to success, in other forms, apply to many other business and non-business activities. Nonetheless, we built this list from the ground up, from our experiences and our discussions, and their wider utility only reinforces their utility for successfully maximizing revenue.

1. Act holistically

The first key to success is not first because it won a bet. It's hard to overestimate the importance of acting holistically in pursuing revenue maximization. Acting holistically has three, equally central meanings: acting through all the functions of the revenue cycle, across all four core strategies, and within the broader business.

Act across functions. With the silo mentality as one of the primary susceptibilities for revenue leakage, it's hardly surprising that a revenue maximization initiative must comprehensively address all functional areas of the company and the revenue cycle to reach its full potential. Yet few companies in the telecom and related industries pursue revenue maximization enterprisewide. A company might tackle billing and network operations, for instance, but not customer care. Or it might address leakage caused by provisioning and customer care but have no cooperation from the IT function.

A company must act across all functions, first, because companies leak across and between functions. Second, and maybe more important, it's necessary to do the job. If a finance executive, for instance, manages a project to reconcile a water utility's metering systems with its billing systems, the project will fail without the expertise, active involvement, and (not to be forgotten) actual data from IT, engineering, and billing functions, each of whom may be resistant to offering help. Companies must also act across functions because it allows them to leverage success. At one company we worked with, the IT function of one legacy company made admirable strategic gains and achieved major financial benefits from revenue maximization. However, because the core project team was buried in one function in one unit, the rest of the organization and other legacy companies did not have a chance to learn from and copy the unit's success.

Link core strategies. As we keep repeating throughout this book, successful revenue maximization programs do not treat each strategy—tools, processes, organizational change, or metrics—as separate initiatives. They knit them together into one indivisible sweater of a strategy: an automated tool leading to processes change, monitoring mechanisms integrated with automated tools, organizational structure shaping process reengineering, and every other permutation and sub-permutation one can imagine. Long term, the true *maximization* of revenue will not come from adding up incremental gains from an automated tool project here and a process change there; full success can only come from an integrated, all-cylinders-firing effort, in which the proverbial sum is greater than parts.

For example, Interland, a leading Web hosting company, launched a major project to stem direct leakage, opportunity leakage, and customer churn. (The project particularly addressed customers who, out of passivity, were failing to renew Interland services.) Interland CFO David Buckel told us that the company "spent an incredible amount of time" on a holistic project over three months that designed new processes and business rules, inspired organizational commitment, automated key areas with new technology solutions, and rigorously measured the project—in other words, interlocked all four of the core strategies.

Integrate into the business. Companies should make revenue maximization decisions *within* the context of everyday business decisions. In terms of resource allocation, this means weighing incremental growth opportunities from this initiative against other growth opportunities. But even if a company pursues revenue maximization outside its normal strategic planning and budgeting process, it will eventually find it impossible to manage the initiative, project by project, without integrating it into broader business decisions. For example, in many industries, back billing unbilled services discovered with a revenue maximization tool is a lip-smacking prospect. It comes with only one little problem: most customers aren't that thrilled about being back billed. So a project must weigh the benefits of immediate capture against customer retention goals.

Revenue maximization concerns must be integrated into many basic business decisions like product design. In the Web services sector, the complexity of products often leads to significant delays in billing and provisioning. When IBM's e-Business hosting services and e-Business on demand unit wanted to capture the opportunity leakage resulting from these delays, it had to completely rethink what services it was selling. Steve Kloeblen, the unit's Director of Finance and Operations, explained to us, "Our unit realized we should simplify IBM's services so that packaged configurations could be easily customized by salespeople and by the customers themselves." "We drove to get a more simplified offering structure," Steve continued, "something that could be handled in the field without having to get a whole engineering team involved in the solution." This approach required product, process, and organizational changes. In a more isolated case in the healthcare industry, considerable leakage from future payment denials and delays originates in manual errors during patient registration. Patient registrars are usually low paid and, as a consequence, registration is often a high turnover area. Deciding whether it's worthwhile to minimize revenue leakage by improving patient registration through investment in training or higher salaries is not a decision that can be made by thinking about revenue leakage in a vacuum. And it's not a decision that can be made by a middle manager solely focused on revenue maximization.

2. See the forest and the trees

To succeed at revenue maximization, a company has to focus equally on the big picture and the little picture. Revenue maximization can be an effective enterprisewide initiative because it encompasses "forest" issues: growth, integrity, profitability, creating shareholder value. More to the point, it is an enterprisewide strategy because it requires cooperation across functions. Yet revenue is actually maximized on the ground. Individual projects address, understand, and correct individual transactions: single charges, single call records, single water meters, single Web hosting customers. Automation allows companies to process and grasp these individual elements, and one of the most important thrusts of revenue maximization is to make these individual elements meaningful through data: collecting new data, massaging old data, looking at data that a company has long measured and ignored, and forcing a company to coolly examine data so it can prevent root causes of inaccuracies. To convert this data successfully into incremental revenue requires piercing focus—focus, for example, on correcting details in an individual process, at an individual airport, or in an individual telecom trunk group.

Some companies we have worked with see only the forest. Top management recognizes the value of revenue maximization and urges it, with a low-energy pep talk, onto the company. But management often doesn't realize that to maximize revenue requires people to roll up their sleeves, address individual details, get down in the mud, and know what they're doing on a technical level. "The complexity of what you find is somewhat daunting," AT&T's Ellyce Brenner shared with us. "One of our work streams is 'integrated usage flow and management' to see if all our usage is flowing into the right places and right systems. Completing the project is requiring *60 tap points* into different systems and a very sophisticated level of processing to capture the revenue. If we didn't have the right subject-matter experts to work with us, we couldn't do it."

Other companies see only the trees. (In some industries in crisis, trees are the only things people think about. As one executive told us, "People are being very tactical right now. They're asking, What do I have to do by noon today? What do I have to do to keep my job?") Within this environment, revenue maximization managers work day in, day out with the individual details but have no sense of the purpose—the goal—of what they are trying to accomplish. This attitude breeds a control orientation (or is bred by one) and almost always prevents major revenue capture. A middle manager at one client was discovering important leaks, but no one would listen to her calls for action because she never made a business case for tackling this problem as a revenue-growth issue. She only described it as an operational issue inside her function.

3. Speak in dollars and cents

Executives we spoke to repeatedly described hurdles to revenue maximization created by other executives at their companies, many deep in a silo mentality, who don't seem to understand the strategy. Their advice for jumping these hurdles is to always speak in dollars and cents, in growth numbers and budgets, in ROI and earnings improvement. Revenue maximization and revenue assurance and revenue cycle enhancement are not difficult concepts to understand, but they (and individual projects like "integrated usage flow management") may feel fuzzy or esoteric to some. "It can still seem like a very abstract opportunity to people in my company," one executive told us. "When I talked to them about reconciling end-to-end the provisioning process, they think it's a scary place to go. But when I tell them that this is a way to meet your budgeted growth goals, that there are processes to do this, that we're in their corner, they understand." Tom Berry and the revenue assurance management function at AT&T experienced tremendous success reducing accounts receivable by launching a program that thoughtfully conveyed—and strategically engaged—the sales organization with clear and quantified messages about how the program was creating value.

In a funny twist, when we spoke to one executive who had deliberately and, exhaustingly talked in dollars and cents to ensure executive buy-in to a revenue maximization initiative, she wistfully reflected that she may have gone overboard. Everyone loved the project she was currently working on, and everybody really loved the project's returns. But no one seemed interested in how her team was doing it. "All they're really concerned about," she said, "is how much money you bring in."

4. Be relentless

If we ever had to choose a revenue maximization mascot, it would be a bulldog, not a brain surgeon. While revenue maximization projects can become knotty and slippery, often requiring IT and engineering assistance, the solution for that knottiness is rarely a conceptual breakthrough. It's usually a doggedness to attack the details, the data, the causes. You have to hang in there. Success in revenue maximization demands relentlessness: a technical relentlessness to count up all the trees and persevere in analyzing and correcting the details and an organizational relentlessness to confront the obstacles of corporate resistance. As Ann Sado of Bell Canada advised, "Sometimes you have to do two or three months of work to get the payback, but when you get the payback, it's a big one."

Success also demands relentlessness to continue pursuing revenue capture after wrong turns. If it's not clear by now, it's worth repeating: many people at first don't like revenue maximization. "Why?" we asked Jeannette Alberte at SBC. "Because it's tough," she answered. "And when things get tough, people run. Because tough stuff means that you got to stick your neck out."

Wrong turns—the tough stuff—happen. In one project we worked on, data from a series of telephone calls was bundled together in order to "re-rate" the calls and make sure that customers were being charged the right amount (in this case, the right discount). Unfortunately, our screen to collect the data inadvertently allowed in call records to which, we later found out, the discount did not apply, such as directory assistance calls. At that point, however, it was too late in the project to go back and unbundle the data.

Relentless people make for relentless initiatives. Revenue maximization requires relentlessness in its champions to ensure relentlessness in its pursuit. Mike McGrath told us that, at that depressing revenue assurance conference in London, he realized that some revenue maximization professionals "don't have organizational clout and some don't have organizational confidence." The initiative's champions need that organization confidence to press ahead and to press ahead *with urgency*. "We didn't have a Kumbaya festival at Bell Canada when we all drank the revenue assurance Kool-Aid," Mike explained. "But we still executed. Every time we went down the road and there was a procedural block, we attacked it another way." Because Mike and his colleagues saw incremental revenue from revenue maximization no differently than revenue from a new product, for instance, they did not throw in the towel during the first round. As he put it, "When a customer says, I don't want to buy something, do you just give up?"

People don't just become relentless if assigned to a task that demands it. Executives we consulted continually reminded us that it's important to select the right people to lead a revenue maximization project. These champions should be gumshoes who enjoy the harder cases, who love to identify and quantify leakage, who judge their professional worth on how much money they can find. The champions should be fighters—"disturbers of the peace," as one executive said—who are willing to, and sort of enjoy, taking on the silo mentality. (Great champions, however, know that breaking down walls sometimes requires fighting and sometimes requires very different skills for forging willing and enthusiastic cooperation.)

Finally, companies must not let the day-to-day challenges avert their eyes from the goal. In *From Good to Great*, Jim

Collins notes the prevalence of a "Stockdale Paradox" at great companies. (Collins named the paradox after a lesson learned from Admiral Jim Stockdale, the highest-ranking prisoner of war in Vietnam.) Collins defines the paradox as the ability to "retain faith that you will prevail in the end, regardless of the difficulties, and at the same time confront the most brutal facts of your current reality, whatever they might be."[1] The high-achieving companies in revenue maximization embody the Stockdale Paradox and take the brutal facts of widespread revenue leakage—its persistence a failure, in many ways, in operating the company—more fully to heart. In the end, they capture more revenue than companies that seem more sanguine about revenue leakage and the challenges of a revenue maximization program.

The challenges can be brutal: bickering from the silos, uncooperative data, a portion of quantified revenue "melting" before it's captured. The compulsively quotable Mike McGrath admitted, "I went through periods when I hated this initiative. It was the most volatile roller-coaster ride in the first year. Not only were you fighting like hell to execute, you also had to fight to get people on board." But Mike always kept the difficulties in perspective. "It's a much easier road to go down," he reflected, "than going into a marketplace where the competition is fierce, where the economy is weakening, and where consumers aren't willing to spend."

5. Do something

In *In Search of Excellence,* the authors listed a "bias for action" as the first attribute of an excellent company. A healthy pragmatism is among the most important keys to success in revenue maximization. Often, when we are asked by resistant companies what they should do first, our response, in unison, is, "Anything." Companies must be willing to make profitable steps even if they're not elegant steps. Too many companies, however, have a bias for *in*action when it comes to revenue maximization. In our experience, companies frequently "admire the problem" and spend month after month studying revenue leakage and doing nothing to eradicate it. One company we know of, seemingly suffering from a classic case of paralysis through analysis, has spent well over a year diagnosing every part of its organization for revenue maximization purposes. It has hired two outside advisors to perform formal diagnostics. Its own highly-skilled core team performed another one. It hasn't yet pulled the trigger on even a mid-sized project.

The dangers of giant leaps. Sometimes, analysis isn't the problem. Sometimes, the solution is the problem. Quite a few companies have invested all their energies into what we call "one giant leap for mankind": a major IT systems upgrade or a long-term process improvement project that will supposedly rid the earth—or at least the company—of inaccuracies and inefficiencies in revenue collection forever. We are skeptical of many of these solutions. For years we've seen leakage stubbornly persist despite the best-laid plans. We have also frequently seen giant leaps take so long to implement, integrate, and optimize that the underlying business has changed by the time the systems are fully operational, and the giant leaps are unable to handle the latest challenges. So too we have seen, in many cases, giant leaps cause more leakage instead of eradicating it.

Even when these giant leap solutions do significantly stem revenue leakage, *they should not replace* a robust and broad strategy of repeated and frequent "small steps." They should, instead, follow the admirable example of IBM, which established a mix of long- and short-term projects in its e-Business hosting area. The area launched a "giant leap" provisioning improvement project that would take 18 months to implement. But, according to Steve Kloeblen, "We didn't wait until the end of that process. We put in a SWAT team to go after immediate revenue capture."

Some companies are, lamentably, content to wait. In the electric utilities industry, for example, much hope has been placed in next-generation meters with greater reliability, functionality, and, especially, ability to collect data in real time. According to our colleagues, however, many utilities use a planned meter replacement strategy as an excuse to do nothing about revenue leakage—failing to go after even the quickest, easiest wins. Particularly troubling is that by attempting to simply plug in greater revenue capture, these companies never create a culture of revenue responsibility or learn the necessary skills of day-to-day process improvement.

Furthermore, many times when we advise companies to pursue revenue maximization projects, they respond that they can't do it right then because they're in the middle of a new systems implementation. Yet, at most companies, there is *always* a new systems implementation. A new implementation, in fact, can be the perfect time to integrate revenue maximization principles and procedures so that improved data quality minimizes leakage.

To err is human. The bias to action—*doing* something—invariably includes a willingness to be disappointed and, frankly, to mess up. Yet, for such notably low-risk initiatives, revenue maximization projects often find themselves smothered by excessive risk-aversion. Many of their champions are simply not used to the quantifiable pressures of formal revenue growth targets.

Of course, the willingness to take risks is usually a function of power. Some managers at larger companies are simply too low on the organizational totem pole to move a resistant organization to action. Senior executives, however, are paid to do this. And occasionally they do. One client, the CFO of a major business unit at a then revenue maximization-resistant company, hired us to perform an initial project. He did so, he explained, on sort of a whim. (He trusted us from a prior relationship.) "I'll give you a shot," he said. Then, with a mischievous smile, he added, somewhat frighteningly, "But if you screw up, I'll come after you."

He never had to come after us.

6. Manage success

The final key to success is about success itself. Some companies have confronted the silo mentality, the control mindset, defensiveness, competition from other priorities, and more with success—a snowballing process of greater and greater success leading to greater and greater commitment leading to greater and greater enthusiasm. But as any schoolchild can tell you, if you roll a pumpkin-sized snowball down a sledding hill, expecting it to get bigger and bigger as snowballs do in cartoons, you'll soon face the hard truth: the ball will either break up or, more likely, get stuck. You can only make a snowball bigger one way: rolling it by hand. For revenue maximizers, we offer three pieces of hand-rolling advice. All are part of an overarching communications strategy that must be conscious, consistent, and well-designed.

Don't overpromise. Some champions fight resistance to revenue maximization initiatives with promises of big, company-changing revenue growth to come. Exuberant vendors and outside advisors sometimes feed this tendency with glitzy—and what they imagine to be mesmerizing—brochures flashing, say, a 15 percent revenue growth opportunity for telecom companies. While this tendency to overstate promises is understandable, it's also dangerous. Initiatives that fail to meet overhyped expectations invite damaging "I told you so's" from the naysayers who pooh-poohed them to begin with. Like many new initiatives, a company will only try revenue maximization once. If the first experience is a big disappointment because of unrealistic expectations, years may go by before a company tries it again.

Avoiding excess exuberance gets easier with experience. As in any type of corporate initiative, companies with mature revenue maximization functions and diverse projects under their belt can much more accurately quantify the opportunities available. Many beginner companies, however, fail to understand the complexity and intricacies of identifying, quantifying, and capturing leaked revenue. For example, we worked with the company whose first project was a reconciliation of its billing system to its client database. Everyone recognized that the opportunity for revenue capture was sizable, but the senior executive overseeing the project was more confident than he should have been given the company's experience. Early on, he committed the project to deliver an aggressive revenue target to the company's overall budget.

Unfortunately, the time allotted for the project was too brief and the underlying data integrity issues too messy for the project to capture the revenue pledged. The executive's promise was broken. (Luckily, the executive authorized the project to continue on a more realistic schedule, and the project eventually delivered over $10 million.)

Celebrate the wins. Successful revenue maximization companies spend considerable time "working the organization" and celebrating the wins, as was done in the article from Bell Canada's internal magazine reprinted in Figure 5.2. Successful champions understand what GE executives call the "social architecture" of their companies.

Figure 5.2
Celebrating the Wins: An Example from Bell Canada's *Bell News*

Celebrating the wins means quantifying the revenue captured and the ROI of individual projects. It means sharing credit with congratulatory e-mails and frequent praise. It means celebrating finding money and never implying that money was lost by someone in the first place. It means never viewing revenue maximization as an audit: the quickest and most effective way to kill this initiative is to make it a witch-hunt or even to imply that someone or some group is at fault. Celebrating the wins means, in essence, getting to a point when people in the company think revenue maximization is, in its own particular way, kind of cool. (Of course, celebrations must be tempered so that they don't produce unrealistic expectations.)

Get quick wins. All snowballs, of course, start with a fist-sized pack of snow, and, in the next few chapters, we repeatedly advise companies to tackle quick-win projects whenever they can. Revenue maximization must be pursued pragmatically, and, for a beginner company, success demands going after the proverbial low-hanging fruit. For example, to help spark greater revenue maximization focus at SBC, Jeannette Alberte managed a pilot project to quantify leakage at only two customers, two large enterprises being billed and processed by dozens of systems throughout the company. As crucial as it is for advanced companies to make steady progress on all four core strategies, we always counsel companies to go after quick wins first, in all areas, immediately. To us, nothing in this world tastes sweeter than low-hanging fruit.

A final note: in many cases, the speed of the snowballing may be in inverse proportion to the size of the company. Smaller, more flexible companies, especially with CEO support, will often be able to make bigger and more energetic initial strides. Larger companies may have to be more methodical in pursuing smaller quick wins, celebrating them, and managing expectations.

The common theme of the six keys of success is leadership—leadership to act holistically, to manage success, to ensure relentlessness, and to *get things done.* Lack of leadership can be dispiriting at companies trying to maximize revenue without it. "We don't have the people who are willing to take risks," an executive at one such company told us. "We don't have the people who will go in and do it, or the people who are able to shake the foundation loose."

We don't want to get teary-eyed, but revenue maximization, like every corporate strategy, isn't done by processes or tools or even "organizations." It's done by people.

Notes

1. Collins, *From Good to Great*, 86.

CHAPTER SIX

WHAT A COMPANY CAN, CAN'T, AND SHOULD DO ITSELF

At the end of each of the next four chapters, we briefly detail recommended "actions a company can take now." *Who* performs these actions often generates a debate. For example, should a company perform an enterprisewide self-diagnostic or hire an outside advisor? Should a company's IT department build software to reconcile systems or purchase external software? In deciding these questions, companies need to keep two things, in particular, in mind. First, they need to ensure objectivity in both the decisions about revenue maximization and in the pursuit of it. Can we, they need to ask themselves, achieve best practices? Can we look at our systems, processes, and people without bias? Second, companies deciding what to do themselves and what to hire others to do must have a strong bias for action. The process of hiring an advisor (or choosing whether to hire an advisor) must not become the project itself, as it has at some companies. Deciding what a company can and can't do itself should be a quick, firm first step. So who should do what? With all self-interest put to the side, we believe **that a company should do as much itself as it possibly can and use outside help selectively and smartly, as kindling when necessary or for leading-edge projects.**

IN PRAISE OF SELF-RELIANCE

In a perfect world, companies would probably not need any outside help for revenue maximization projects, with the possible exception of some leading-edge software tools. Many companies have considerable skill and experience in designing processes, effecting organizational change management, and installing tools. We have also found that many people involved in revenue maximization at these companies are coiled springs, whose talents explode when their efforts are recognized. There is no hard and fast reason why ambitious companies shouldn't be able to do most revenue maximization activities themselves. They can, for example, benchmark themselves if they aggressively do their homework by attending industry conferences and frequently engaging in informal intercompany dialogues. Many companies have impressive IT departments, which can—if committed—design first-generation, invaluable automated tools.

A company should do as much as it can in-house for a few reasons:

- The obvious reason in an initiative frequently starved for resources: cost.

- The sage chestnut, don't outsource your problems. If outside advisors or vendors perform the bulk of the work without significant company staff involvement, little knowledge transfer will occur, and the company will never institutionalize the skills necessary for ongoing revenue capture.
- If only an outside party is on the hook for revenue maximization, the broad and deep *commitment* to revenue maximization so necessary for success will never infiltrate the organization.
- At some companies, outsiders can ruffle feathers. That's not always bad, but it can occasionally do more harm than good.
- Outside advisors come with risks. Some (no names, please) aren't that good. (Companies should be especially wary of desperate advisors or vendors who overpromise. The surest warning sign is a promise of totally pain-free gain.)

Help is available

If the world were perfect, companies could do everything themselves. In this world, outside advisors and vendors are often necessary to serve as kindling to catalyze revenue maximization initiatives. They also bring to the table real, advanced, accelerating skills.

Using advisors as kindling doesn't mean setting them on fire. (Even the most boring and wooden of us aren't that flammable.) It means recognizing, for whatever sociopsychological reason, that outsiders often serve as effective catalysts for revenue maximization, especially at companies that tend to admire the problem instead of taking action and at companies that tend to get tangled in bureaucratic knots.

"A trusted third-party detailing the revenue opportunity was the biggest driver for others outside the revenue assurance function to open their eyes," one executive told us. Another said, "It really took bringing in a well-known consulting firm and shelling out the bucks to get attention at the company. Sometimes, in a large corporation, you get better credence through an outside, independent opinion."

Outside advisors can serve as good initial catalysts because they can often complete projects faster than internal teams; speed in achieving quick wins is crucial during the early stages of revenue maximization. Advisors frequently bring a discipline and a tenacity to the tasks of finding and capturing revenue—a tenacity that's been even more evident since many consultants have started writing in bonus clauses tied to incremental revenue captured. (Their potential clients, however, should examine their own motivation for engaging advisors for contingency projects. If the company is doing this because it doesn't have any resources or "corporate will" to dedicate to revenue maximization, it is probably better not to hire the advisor on contingency in the first place. Little would have been accomplished anyway.)

Outside advisors do more than get a fire started. They bring real skills and, the single most important benefit, *experience*. A company can do a diagnostic itself, but an outside party is probably more aware of industry best practices. A company can complete almost every revenue maximization project on its own, for sure—companies do it all the time—but an advisor who has done similar projects again and again at other companies will know where to look, how to overcome data challenges, and how to convert information into fixes. IT departments can write code to reconcile systems, but a software vendor dedicated exclusively to this task will almost certainly bring more powerful and user-friendly functionality. And the automated tool won't have to dwell for months in an already packed waiting room.

Outsiders first, then onto capture. In general, *outsiders are more appropriate for finding and quantifying leakage than for capturing it.* Rigorous methodologies, familiarity with automated tools, and a nose for leaks developed through experience can accelerate the identification and measurement of inaccuracies in collecting all the revenue and only the revenue they deserve. But preventing these inaccuracies in the long term usually requires the re-engineering of major processes, the ongoing management of preventive tools, and constant organizational diligence, all skills that are best done in-house by people who understand the particular ecology of their company.

We recommend bringing in outside advisors selectively and smartly, primarily, in our opinion, when a company is pushing into new areas. One exasperated telecom senior executive we met with once declared, "I'm sick of hearing about low-hanging fruit. Someone get me a [bleeping] ladder." Advisors can be that [bleeping] ladder. Good ones will also ensure a skill transfer so that companies can apply the lessons, strategies, and actual tools of once leading-edge projects more routinely in other areas of the organization.

Not all advisors have to work outside the company. Six Sigma companies are famous for their "Black Belt" training—where a central team trains "the best and the brightest" in Six Sigma strategies, analysis, and tactics so that these certified Black Belts can take these strategies back to their operations.[1] In some advanced revenue maximization companies like Verizon and Bell Canada, the corporate revenue maximization function is evolving into an in-house consultancy, collecting best practices from inside and outside the firm and applying this expertise to various business units.

Obviously, a company faces a constant trade off between doing as much as it can itself and leveraging outside help. Sometimes the tradeoffs are difficult to weigh. For instance, the finance area of one telecom company we know of wanted to hire an advisor to quantify provisioning-related leakage. The company's IT function became alarmed, insisting that *it* could do the project better and more cheaply. The function didn't even know the details of the project, and it took three weeks to deliver a work plan, one that estimated nine months of effort instead of the advisor's estimate of three. To this day, we're not sure whether it would have been better to have actually hired the advisors or to never have engaged them in the first place.

NOTES

1. Welch, *Jack: Straight from the Gut,* 332.

CHAPTER SEVEN

DAY-TO-DAY PROCESSES

One project we worked on produced some of the quickest and most gratifying revenue maximization success we've seen. An international wireless telecom company had assigned revenue maximization-like responsibilities to a team in its billing function and a team in its network function. For one particular type of error held in suspense—an error regularly "coughed out" by the system because the call record was incomplete—the network team assumed that the billing team was reviewing and correcting the error, and—insert double take here—the billing team assumed that the network team was doing so. The problem went on for two years. It was corrected in a day.

If only all successes were that easy...

Interestingly, the problem arose for an almost no-fault reason: as the wireless company was building up its network, the network system didn't have the capacity to handle the category of error records. The company had programmed the system to "cough out" the errors into a special file. But even after the network reached sufficient capacity to process the records, no one ever revisited the procedure.

This would not have happened if the company had executed the first core strategy, **integrating revenue maximization into day-to-day processes**. Then, it would have regularly documented, analyzed, and improved processes to make sure the company collected the revenue it deserved for the services it had provided.

Day-to-day processes are the series of tasks, steps, rules, and decisions—the methods and procedures (M&Ps) as they're often called—that a company follows in everything it does, including making sure its revenue collection is timely, accurate, and complete. Flaws in revenue-related processes occur all the time. A task is handed off to another area in an uncontrolled, unchecked manner. Work steps or business rules aren't defined. No one is held accountable for a work step. A procedure is missing, especially between functions.

In our work and our colleagues' work, the "a-ha" moments—those obvious, smack-yourself-on-the-forehead moments—of major, low investment revenue capture has frequently come from the easy correction of these easily correctible process flaws. (One telecom carrier, for instance, discovered a responsibility gap costing the company $7 million per year.) Integrating revenue maximization into day-to-day processes can be one of the easiest things to do to maximize revenue. It can be as simple as adding a single work step or a clearer business rule.

Integrating revenue maximization into day-to-day processes can also be a company's *most difficult, maddening* challenge. Ten years ago, "process reengineering" was a magazine-cover issue as companies analyzed their overall processes to discover where costs (and boatloads of people) could be removed. We believe that many companies need to undergo a similar exercise to improve profitability, bolster integrity, and capture the opportunity within through revenue maximization. They don't need to do it tomorrow, perhaps, but in the long term, to succeed, companies need to summon the stamina and leadership needed to dive into the thick, suffocating, overgrown swamp of day-to-day processes that have developed organically over the years as a result of short-term decisions and actions.

We remember a consultant who spoke at a revenue assurance conference a few years ago. The gentleman theatrically announced that he had "*the* most important revenue assurance tool" in his "magic box." He did have a magic box on stage, although it didn't look particularly magical to us. Nevertheless, after a fifteen-minute teasing speech (we were thinking, "Enough already, Houdini, open up the box)," the consultant lifted the lid of his magic box and revealed… a pencil. (We were hoping for a ray gun or something.) Actually, we thought, "Corny but true. Process change, redesign, and definition starts—and sometimes ends—with a pencil." The actions begun with the pencil can lead to capturing millions of dollars because, by integrating revenue maximization into day-to-day processes, a company directly addresses the proximate causes of revenue leakage: in faulty processes themselves and in repeated human errors that are the functions of poor processes. Companies and advisors, however, have often ignored process improvement because these projects tend to be, on the relative scale of revenue maximization, less glamorous. Gains from these projects are also often harder to measure than those produced by technology-related initiatives.

THE FIVE KEY FEATURES OF DAY-TO-DAY PROCESSES

As illustrated in Figure 7.1, there are five key features for a best-practice revenue maximization process improvement strategy:

1. **Clearly defined work steps and business rules**
2. **Individual management and accountability**
3. **Measurability of results**
4. **Elimination of duplication and gaps**
5. **Integration of revenue maximization processes into** *all change*

Figure 7.1
Key Features of a Day-to-Day Processes Strategy

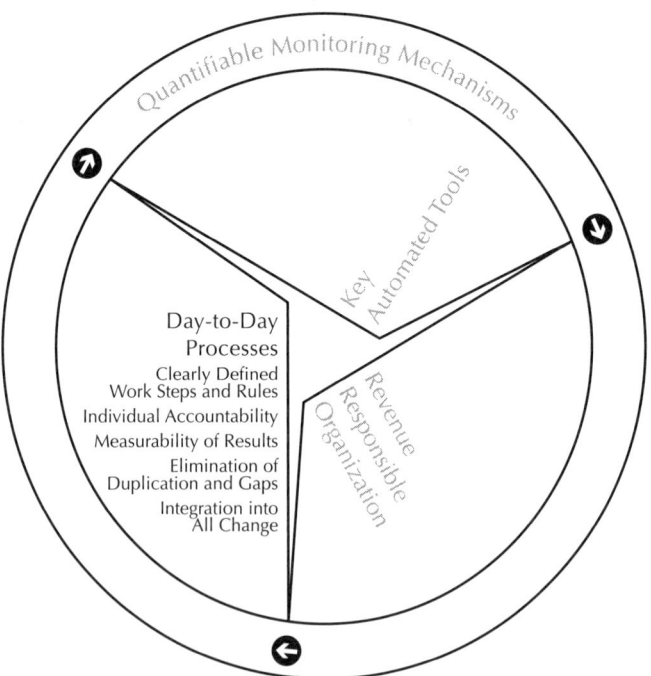

STRATEGY FEATURES: CLEARLY DEFINED
WORK STEPS AND BUSINESS RULES

Few people, we have found, dispute the importance of these features. They just ask, "Who has the time?"

Well, make the time.

1. CLEARLY DEFINED WORK STEPS AND BUSINESS RULES

A best-practice revenue maximization company will have clearly defined work steps and business rules. Most companies, however, to capture more revenue, have to put "define" in the present tense and work to more clearly define the steps and rules.

Poorly controlled, undefined, or simply stale work steps and business rules cause revenue leakage and, more broadly, the inaccurate collection of revenue. Ardent revenue maximizers swap stories of whoppers—egregious leakage due to process flaws—like old Vermont yankees trading examples of dumb things said by vacationing New Yorkers. For example, one regional electric utility had installed huge wholesale electric meters at its major customers. The company later discovered that, because of unclear (or ignored) work steps, paperwork sometimes took three months to make its way from hand to hand and into the billing system to generate bills.

Companies must exert energy to document processes and proactively define work steps and business rules (and all M&Ps, for that matter) *for the purpose of maximizing revenue.* This applies to processes conducted by a revenue maximization function itself and processes throughout the revenue cycle, especially in areas identified as causing leakage. This involves a wide range of activities: inserting new work steps, better defining business rules, keeping processes from getting stale, getting processes on paper, and reengineering whole processes from a revenue maximization perspective. Doing all this enables a company, first, to "fix" things—that is, to eliminate process causes of leakage—and then, to do more: to incorporate new, best-practice revenue maximizing *controls* into the way a company does business.

Insert new work steps to maximize revenue. Sometimes definition means addition. If, for example, a revenue maximization project reveals consistent errors in a master rate table (or a charge description master, as it's called in healthcare), adding a new work step to minimize misinterpretations of a marketing function's instructions is often a necessary control step. Similarly, our colleagues have worked with healthcare companies' frontline registration employees to implement straightforward new process steps based on "toolkits" that clearly communicate key third-party payer information, like co-payment requirements and non-covered services, to improve registration accuracy and minimize denied payments.

Of course, companies must find a happy medium when contemplating new work steps. They must be mindful not to foster an overly controlling environment or develop a sclerotic bureaucracy. They must also weigh the costs of inserting new work steps. Many hospitals, for instance, have constructed mature and successful processes to minimize revenue leakage from long inpatient stays. They haven't done the same for lower-value outpatient services. Alexander Cibenko of Saint Vincent Catholic Medical Centers of New York explained to us, "On the inpatient side, if we have to collect $100,000 on an account, we make sure that we have the proper pre-registration, insurance verification, data collection, and billing processes in place. People understand what they have to do to be able to collect the revenue. And

STRATEGY FEATURES: CLEARLY DEFINED WORK STEPS AND BUSINESS RULES

volumes associated with inpatient stays are manageable." For outpatient care, Alex said, "You may have a $200 or a $400 or a $23 account. Yet you have all the same work, coverage and admission clearance requirements needed as for inpatient care. The question then becomes, how much cost are we willing to bear to collect on these small balance accounts." So far, across the industry, hospitals haven't put forth the same effort to create rigorous revenue maximization processes for these lower-value services, and the accumulation of leaked revenue from smaller accounts is having a major, negative financial impact.

We have found that one of the most wanting (and thus most fruitful) areas for creating new, more rigorous work steps is in contract management, especially at companies that rely on large contracts with a few major customers. In the telecom industry, we worked on a project to improve the revenue capture of a long-haul fiber optic carrier's multi-million dollar, extremely complex contracts. There was no standard structure for these contracts and no repeatable work steps. The contracts weren't even stored in one place. Some amendments to the contracts were not written down but were rather "gentlemen's agreements" between the sales function and the customer. Individual salespeople were in charge of invoicing, and some did the task with little effort. We helped identify and quantify $30 million of revenue leakage arising from poor contract management and assisted the company in developing formal ownership of the contract process, specific M&Ps for contract management, and a plan to install IT systems to better handle contracts.

At technology services company Pegasus Solutions, Ed Barnes, the company's vice president and controller, told us of similar gains from better processes in the contract area. "A lot of our contracts call for increases every year tied to the Consumer Price Index [CPI]," Ed explained. "But we didn't have formal and rigorous processes for the CPI increase. Some of our systems provided notice, but some of them didn't alert us about these CPI increases. We have now scheduled a quarterly formal process to manage these increases." Pegasus has also instituted more rigorous processes to, among other goals, charge interest on delinquent payments, renew contracts, manage short payments, and manage work orders.

Define needed business rules. Some people think of processes as extraordinarily complex tendons weaving through a corporation that appear, only occasionally, as inscrutable flow charts. Processes are like that sometimes, but more often they are simply rules. Defining business rules is crucial to maximizing revenue. For example, at a Web hosting company our team worked with, contracts included stipulations to charge for specific types of calls to the tech-support desk. Yet the division's tech support people, often in a spirit of easy-going customer service, almost *never* routed tickets for ultimate charge capture. (To be exact, they routed tickets about 0.5 percent of the time.) This cost the company millions in leaked revenue. To arrest the leakage, the company began a long-term "entitlement management" project to more clearly define tech-support charges in the original contracts and to establish clearer business rules for its tech-support people about when they must charge. (The company attacked the problem on a second, cultural front to shift, in the words of the executive in charge of the project, the organization from a "full—service mentality" to a "product-oriented mentality.")

STRATEGY FEATURES: CLEARLY DEFINED WORK STEPS AND BUSINESS RULES 127

Keep processes from getting stale. Clearly defining work steps and business rules is not a one-time task. Processes to prevent inaccuracies in revenue collection, like houseguests, can get old quickly and need to be frequently reviewed to make sure that they are relevant and useful. Some companies do frequently review and update processes and controls. For example, at GTE, now part of Verizon, "Every employee had to go through gap training and continuous process improvement training," according to Karin Wagar.

However, many companies conducted major, systematic day-to-day process documentation projects ten years ago and now find that the older, corrected processes have been interwoven with or paved over by new ones. (And the process-improvement project's phone book-thick summary report is now about as relevant as a decade-old list of employees.) We worked with one telecom company to document M&Ps related to adjustment claims from its CLEC customers. Company management was comfortable that CLEC claims were low. Yet the project found that 99 percent of the claims had actually never been registered in the proper systems. The claims were being entered with expired codes from different M&Ps.

We occasionally experience other "night of the living dead process" scenes. During one telecom company diagnostic, we interviewed a midlevel clerk responsible for end-to-end reconciliation of some of the company's systems. She proudly showed us her elaborate computer model for "revenue assurance." We nodded. It did have an awful lot of fields to enter. But it didn't point to any leakage or uncover any root causes. We pushed her for two hours on an obvious question: how could this one company, alone in the whole world, not find inaccuracies when it reconciled its systems?

She didn't know: "Uh, maybe we're good." Finally, we left the office, baffled and defeated. Only later did we figure out—we're not always so quick—that the woman's work steps were stale. She wasn't reconciling one system to the next. She was reconciling the front page of one system's periodic report to its last page. She was doing arithmetic.

Get processes on paper. Revenue maximization-related activities in the dabbler and pre-dabbler phases are usually scattered throughout a company under many different names. Routine control and leakage-prevention activities get done, of course—companies aren't leaking 50 percent of revenue—but they are often not part of an individual's formal responsibilities. Big Phil at XYZ Corp, for example, may make it his responsibility to keep an eye on one category of exceptions. Little Tony, a product manager, is proud that he's always thinking about the billing implications of a new service launch. As important as this ad hoc concern for leakage often is, *revenue maximization processes must be documented to prevent the personalization of work steps.*

First, companies grow, and casual revenue maximization activities often cannot adapt to the more complicated processes of a larger organization. This has been a problem in the technology services industry. With companies merging frequently and expanding quickly to meet demand, "You can't rely on the guys down the hall anymore," explained Barbara Gibson, vice president of Interland. "In our industry, there are lots of problems with inconsistent hand-offs from one department to the next." Second, people leave companies, especially the senior middle managers who have most likely been performing informal control steps. Finally, in business, anything can happen. People occasionally die. At one company we know of, the "guy who did revenue assurance" passed away in his sleep one night. Unfortunately, no one had any idea what he had been doing while he was alive. It took months for the company to reconstruct his activities and restart even basic control procedures. More problematic, it turned out that he hadn't been doing a whole series of obvious and necessary steps to maximize revenue for reasons, as the saying goes, that he took to his grave.

Reengineering processes to maximize revenue. Clearly defining work steps and business rules often occurs at the end of a discrete revenue maximization project. At that point, leakage has been quantified and a new work step or rule has become part of the capture plan. Yet, because whole companies and whole processes are leaky, projects are often needed to better define *all* work steps and business rules. Companies may have to add a new series of controls—extra steps or rules—into some processes or simplify others that are too complex. If, for example, a provisioning center seems prone to error, a company should analyze the steps of each frontline provisioning operator and look at these steps through a revenue maximization lens to understand and improve work flow, operator scripts, provisioning system interfaces, and post-customer interaction procedures.

Leading companies do this. Detroit's Henry Ford Health Systems, according to an article in *Healthcare Financial Management*, launched a major process reengineering project to standardize processes across all points of services and implement new processes and business rules, such as providing financial consulting services earlier in a patient's visit. The benefits in the first ten months of the program included $9.2 million in additional net revenue, a 52 percent decrease in registration-related denials of third-party payments, and a

30 percent increase in point-of-service cash collection. (The project also enabled the organization, in a prime example of efficiency capture, to move 10 central billing office employees from rework and error correction to more value-added functions.)[1]

Some companies hope that a major automated technology solution can spare them the sweat and pain of a difficult process improvement project. Steve Kloeblen warned against this. "Manual processes are a real problem," he told us. Steve's business units at IBM, for example, suffered considerable opportunity leakage at one point from delays between sales and billing. "We found in some places that it took five or six or seven different functions between when we recognized a billable event and when we got the bill out the door." IBM, naturally, looked at automation solutions. But Steve argued, "If you automate the function, you're just paving the cow path. Instead, we've figured out ways to improve, for instance, our sales process efficiency 100 percent in the time it takes a proposal to get to a customer. We're targeting three or four times improvement just through other process changes." Tools play a role, Steve believes, but they are part of the solution. "Tools solidify process change."

2. INDIVIDUAL MANAGEMENT AND ACCOUNTABILITY

When we argued above against personalizing revenue maximization responsibility—Big Phil or Little Tony just kind of doing stuff—we weren't arguing against individualizing processes. In fact, we recommend the opposite. The second key feature of integrating revenue maximization into day-to-day processes is to ensure individual management and

STRATEGY FEATURES: INDIVIDUAL MANAGEMENT AND ACCOUNTABILITY

accountability. Companies must bring the documentation of day-to-day revenue maximization processes to an individual level, to corporate positions (a network manager or a vice president of IT), with clear responsibilities assigned.

First and most immediately, this means bringing relevant M&Ps to individuals' formal work plans and job responsibilities: an electric meter installer, for example, must follow five specific steps to ensure that a newly-installed meter is registered on a utility's systems. Sometimes, individual management means creating new M&Ps. Thus, for the healthcare desktop toolkits for patient registration, our colleagues advised developing "toolkit champions" to keep the various toolkits updated with insurer and managed care information.

Revenue maximization must keep its own house in order, and project teams should apply *above-average* thoughtfulness and rigor to ensure thorough individual accountability for revenue maximization projects and functional tasks. But individual accountability also has a broader meaning: an attempt to distribute individual management and accountability throughout the organization, into the processes of all corporate functions necessary to capture leaked revenue, and into all the processes of corporate functions that leak revenue (in other words, the whole enchilada).

Ensuring individual management requires that processes and procedures are not relegated to large books, that sit idly on shelves. Job-level M&Ps must be constantly updated. A few leading companies have had success using Web-based technologies to distribute and keep job-level processes fresh. One company we worked with instituted a policy that its Web-based process descriptions, every month, had to either be confirmed as relevant or updated.

Ellyce Benner of AT&T stressed to us the importance of "creating a cultural norm to make revenue, revenue recovery, and revenue assurance everyone's job at the corporation." This cultural norm is absolutely critical. So are M&Ps that actually make revenue maximization everyone's job at the corporation.

3. Measurability of results

In Chapter 10, we detail our case for the strategic importance of quantifiable monitoring mechanisms. The building blocks of these monitoring mechanisms are metrics applied on an individual, process-by-process basis. Companies should actively measure the revenue implications of key processes. How many incorrectly ticketed exchanges, for example, does an airline's current process produce? How many payment denials originate in errors made in a hospital's patient registration? As Pat Walker of Qwest explained, "If you don't have metrics, it's hard to see where the flaws in the process are. They're so hand in glove that it's hard to separate them." Nonetheless, most telecom companies have done little in terms of measuring the revenue leakage from individual processes.

Measurability of results also applies to process-improvement *projects*. Companies must verify the ROI and quantify the revenue capture of revenue maximization projects. Many formal initiatives do this, even if few do it as rigorously or in as an enterprisewide a way as GE, where a financial analyst certifies the results of every Six Sigma project.[2]

The importance of measurability of results to integrating revenue maximization into day-to-day processes also applies on an individual basis. It's difficult to conceive of a way to

STRATEGY FEATURES: ELIMINATION OF DUPLICATION OR GAPS

ensure accountability on an individual level without measuring processes for which individuals are accountable. Day-to-day processes must be measured across the board, from operational metrics for frontline employees (how many meters are correctly installed, for instance), to financial metrics for the people upstairs (how much money is the company leaking due to its metering processes).

4. ELIMINATION OF DUPLICATION OR GAPS

Clearly-defined work steps and business rules, individual accountability, and measurability of results could apply to a wide variety of process improvement initiatives—processes to improve regulatory compliance or cut costs or enhance health and safety performance. The final two key features of this core strategy are thrusts—areas of focus—that address process situations that frequently cause revenue leakage. The first one, eliminating process duplication and gaps, has been one of the most robust and remunerative sources of preventive revenue capture in the industries we have worked with.

Mind the gap. The danger of gaps in day-to-day revenue maximization processes is self-evident. No one is correcting a recurring source of leakage. At an electric utility, for example, five different functions will often deal with meters. Our colleagues found huge gaps at one utility in day-to-day processes to install new automated meters. Nearly $4 million per year was falling through the cracks because all meters weren't being tracked in the system. The company installed some meters with no record of installation and some with inaccurate information, mainly because of the poor hand-off of tasks between functions.

Frequently, we encounter telecom companies with gap-ridden sales promotion processes. A company, for instance, will launch an "Everybody Must Call Wait" sale, offering call waiting for a nickel for the first two months. This is all very nice, except when no function accepts responsibility for turning off the promotion code that generates the bill at the nickel-per-month rate. Quite reasonably, the customer care function, which may have signed up customers for the promotion, claims that changing rates is a back office issue. The billing area argues that the sales and marketing function, which designed the goofy program in the first place, ought to be responsible for the end-to-end process and assign its resources to switch customers to the correct price. This kind of public bickering is actually productive in the rare cases it happens. At most companies, the gap in turning off the promotion code persists because everyone just assumes, without discussion, that handling the task is another function's responsibility.

Gaps are also prevalent in outsourcing relationships, in which a company, like one electric utility we know of, assumed that the partner to whom it had outsourced its billing function had accepted responsibility for basic revenue collection controls. It hadn't. A telecom company wanted to initiate a project to reconcile its data about call usage with its billing data to maximize revenue. Yet the company no longer "owned" the data because it had outsourced billing operations. The situation got extraordinarily complicated when the company switched outsourcing vendors and the old vendor refused to cooperate with the revenue maximization project, leaving unbridgeable gaps in the attempts at data reconciliation.

STRATEGY FEATURES: ELIMINATION OF DUPLICATION OR GAPS

Duplication: when one hand is better than two. The efficiency capture opportunities of eliminating duplication of revenue maximization processes are clear, both in terms of cost savings and the ability to convert once-duplicated resources into value-added drivers of revenue maximization. Few companies enjoy employing people who add little or no value to the enterprise, except maybe family-owned businesses that need a place to safely hide ne'er-do-well nephews.

Duplication is persistent. In the telecom industry, for example, despite rounds and rounds of layoffs, companies still have pockets of "checkers checking checkers," in the words of Terry Mosey. A group of clerks, for instance, may audit master rate tables that go into a system and a group of bill checkers will spend considerable amounts of time calculating whether the already-checked rates are correct. These rates are frequently incorrect, but the problem demands process improvement and automated tools at the front end where the errors occur. The final bill checkers, for this part of the process, are simply wasting resources. While we've often seen wrong rates go into a billing system, we've never seen correct rates go into a billing system and come out wrong.

Most duplicated processes aren't as obvious as checkers checking checkers—or they aren't obvious to a company that's been doing things a certain way for as long as anyone can remember. The duplication of processes can be detrimental in a more subtle way, such as when similar processes are duplicated at individual business units or geographical divisions. We do not recommend that every company install a Global Command Center for every process—insurance reimbursement processing, for instance, or customer collections—but many companies that have centralized processes have discovered tremendous benefits from tighter control, clearer day-to-day process management, operating efficiencies, and faster implementation of best practices. Our colleagues, for example, have worked with healthcare company MedPartners to redesign a corporate business office in Alabama where the staff was organized into clusters representing geographic regions and cells representing physician specialties to ensure best-practice process to bill, follow up on billing, and respond to customer inquiries.

5. INTEGRATE REVENUE MAXIMIZATION PROCESSES INTO ALL CHANGE

The final feature of process improvement is to integrate clear, measurable, accountable revenue maximization processes into all change. Almost every executive we talked to about revenue maximization (for this book and in general) at some point gets a faraway look in his or her eyes, sighs, and says, "I wish we had just done this from the beginning." Revenue maximization should sit at the table from day one when new systems, new products, or new acquisitions are designed or contemplated—in fact, when any major business decision is made. Change causes leaks, and companies must be vigilant and *proactive* in integrating revenue maximization, specific M&Ps, and best-practice controls into all change.

Some companies are doing this. One telecom executive we spoke to told us about her previous job at a leading financial services company. At that company, an important and highly-respected "financial control" group worked with the IT and product development organizations on every major change. The financial control group followed rigorous processes: it analyzed reports, system outputs, and system inputs and ensured, before products were launched, that the company would accurately and immediately capture all the revenue and only the revenue it deserved. Many companies, however, aren't doing this regularly, or at all. If these companies continue to exclude revenue maximization from change, they will, regardless of their other revenue maximization initiatives, not capture the profitability, integrity, and growth opportunities from within their companies.

Processes for new products. The accelerated pace of product development is a major cause of revenue leakage and a major impediment to companies trying to capture the full economic value of new products. Documented best-practice processes can ensure maximum revenue capture from the gate. To many new product teams, additional processes may seem obstructive and "bureaucratic," but many speedy launches routinely lose in leakage what they gain in speed.

Tom Berry of AT&T told us, "Generally at telecom companies in a rush to go to market, there can be a tendency to do things quickly, bypassing systematic ways of doing things, doing a lot of manual processes, and relying on individuals rather than processes—sometimes individuals who change jobs." At AT&T, Tom's revenue assurance management area is continually striving to improve the integration of revenue maximization processes into new products. This isn't easy. "For us," Tom shared, "scale is a key challenge for revenue assurance. If a program or product is wildly successful in the incubator phase, once it goes into 'full production,' we want to make sure that everything in the early stage doesn't fall out, resulting in lost bills or an excessive amount of back billing."

As tough as the challenges can be, meeting them head-on is necessary. U.S. Cellular, for example, has integrated revenue maximization processes into all change. According to an article in *Wireless Review,* John Quille, Corporate

Controller at U.S. Cellular, assembles an interdepartmental revenue maximization team to write a "project rollout plan"—a plan that sits beside the marketing plan—which considers the implications of all major initiatives for employee training, revenue control, and revenue-recording procedures. The U.S. Cellular team has also developed a checklist to manage methodically how *other* processes and systems will be affected by a new initiative.[3]

Whatever the specific processes for preventing leakage, it is important, at some level, simply to draw a line in the sand. One telecom company we spoke to found that billing at minimally acceptable levels of accuracy, completeness, and timeliness often lagged product launches by six or seven months. The company, in the executive's words, eventually made a firm decision to "just not go to market unless we can bill customers right and the systems are in place."

Processes for new systems. Integrating revenue maximization processes into change also requires developing, hiring, or assigning subject-matter experts who understand how specific types of changes, especially IT and engineering changes, will affect revenue collection and revenue maximization processes. Rigorous M&Ps and engaged experts, for example, could have helped the hospitals discussed in Chapter 3 avoid the billing system-triggered crises that befell them.

Day-to-day processes for system changes must also include a full understanding of how a particular system works within the revenue cycle. As odd as it may seem, considering the basic revenue implications—understanding how specific services will make money—is not a natural process step in many IT- and engineering-led changes. At one telecom company we worked with, a certification procedure for new switches did not encompass robust revenue-related work steps. The network function only tested if a switch routed a call correctly, not if it recorded the call correctly for billing purposes. After the company discovered the resulting leakage, it had to test and fix each switch in an expensive process, the largest cost of which was, of course, the now unrecoverable money that had leaked. The company has since implemented new work steps and controls to ensure that future switch certification projects do not cause the same problems.

Actions a company can take now

Here and at the end of the next three chapters, we include a brief section on what actions a company can take now to implement a particular core strategy. We realize that, like a Las Vegas blackjack dealer laying out the cards, we have rapidly, breathlessly, dealt out best practices for integrating revenue maximization into day-to-day processes. So we offer the following more concrete projects and areas of focus. We list these projects, generally, in order from the easiest—those for companies with no experience with revenue maximization—to the hardest for those companies already deeply committed to the initiative.

1. **Keep your house in order.** Those managing a revenue maximization initiative must make a particular effort to document and establish best-practice, clear, measurable, and accountable M&Ps for their own activities. This applies to companies that have created a formal revenue maximization function and to those who (less ideally) have only assembled an ad hoc task force.

2. **Integrate revenue maximization day-to-day processes into the next product launch.** Unless a company uses outside help, its first experience integrating revenue maximization into a product launch (or, for that matter, a systems change) will be more about learning than doing. Starting a program of integrating revenue maximization into changes will help a company begin to develop repeatable M&Ps to minimize revenue collection inaccuracies from sloppy, rushed, or just plain dumb processes.

3. **Go for a quick win in a process area.** The advice of Pete Varley at Bell Canada on day-to-day process projects is to "start smart, small, and simple." Bell Canada's first major revenue maximization process improvement project was in its consumer division in Ontario. "We took a fair bit of criticism for starting in the 'easier' consumer division," Pete recalled. "But processes are complex. So taking a simpler, more established market like consumer enabled us to prove to other businesses that the goal was there."

Where do you find a quick-win process project? Some quick wins come from an enterprisewide diagnostic. Some may become evident after an afternoon's work of brainstorming with the magic box's not-so-magic pencil. But many, if not most, discrete day-to-day process improvement projects follow, as naturally as night follows day, automated tool projects launched to detect revenue leakage.

4. **Document high-level processes in one leak-prone area.** To really integrate revenue maximization into day-to-day processes, a company must go beyond inserting additional control steps or better defining

business rules. It must document its entire revenue cycle and all of its processes related to collecting revenue and at the some point reengineer them to maximize that collection. "Whoa there, buddy," people invariably say to us when we mention this. "Sorry to say," we respond. "This, longterm, is a must." As difficult as it is, as daunting as it may seem, most companies, we have found, have institutional skills—or at least institutional experience—to formally document key processes.

This is only a first step. We've yet to say anything about how actually to reengineer a process. The hundreds of books written about the topic provide important guidance and concrete methodologies. (Most of these books, alas, also provide wonderful cures for insomnia. Consult a few of them anyway.) The books usually recommend some variation of a commonsense approach to process improvement:

- Document existing processes.
- Analyze those processes by benchmarking them against best practices.
- Prioritize what you need to change.
- Change it.
- Institutionalize process change so processes continually evolve to address underlying business changes.

We advise companies to start the first step—documenting processes—by focusing on one key leak-prone area. A company can do this at a highlevel by looking only at major decision points and responsibilities. It can do it at the nitty-gritty level of individual work steps and specific hand-offs. (This is the kind of process project that produces flowcharts that fill rooms and swallow small towns.) Documenting processes is a time-consuming task in itself, but it serves two important functions. First, it often immediately reveals missing work steps or glaring gaps, thus pointing to quick and easy preventive revenue capture. Second, it begins to institutionalize the rigor necessary for a larger day-to-day process improvement program. Companies, however, should probably not invest any resources in documenting processes if they do not plan on acting on the results. Projects that stop at analyzing processes will not produce tangible gains and will often taint a revenue maximization initiative with the reputation for being a bureaucratic waste of time.

5. **Thoroughly diagnose duplication and gaps.** Companies, at some point, must look at all their major processes and identify and correct areas where duplication or gaps lead to inefficiencies or revenue leakage.

6. **Begin reengineering *all* revenue-related processes to integrate revenue maximization goals, starting in the most leak-prone areas.** Although this action is, by now, self-explanatory, we must note, once again, its difficulty and importance. Altering crotchety, sticky, tangled-up processes is a challenge, and maybe a nightmare. But companies do it every day. Some enthusiast companies have reengineered significant swaths of day-to-day processes to maximize revenue and have generated real value. For all companies, constant process improvement and process redesign

skills must become, as the authors of *The Six Sigma Way* assert, "a critical core competency for 21st-century organizations."[4]

NOTES

1. Robert J. Schneider, Sheldon P. Mandelbaum, Ken Graboys, and Cynthia Bailey, "Process-Centered Revenue-Cycle Management Optimizes Payment Process," *Healthcare Financial Management*, (1 January 2001), 63.

2. Welch, *Jack: Straight from the Gut*, 331.

3. Deborah Young, "Finding the Money," *Wireless Review*, (31 July 2000.)

4. Pande, Neuman, and Cavanagh, *The Six Sigma Way*, 287.

CHAPTER EIGHT

Key Automated Tools

Most revenue maximization projects aren't fodder for the *Harvard Business Review*. They may not be the stuff of outdoor adventure magazines either, but individual projects share more with hiking up a mountain than with soft-chair exercises in deep thinking. Revenue maximization projects demand technical skill, of course, but even more, they demand hard work, relentlessness, and diligence. Diligence is especially needed in the many projects that leverage automated tools, a technology that in some cases has developed an unfair reputation for being mysterious or esoteric.

It's not. **Implementing key automated tools is not only a core strategy of revenue maximization but also an early step in some of the most straightforward projects to maximize revenue.** For example, "provision check," as we call it—others do similar projects under an equally creative name—

is one of the most powerful and useful automated tool projects in the telecom, Web services, and cable industries. (In the last four years, provisioning projects we've been involved with around the world have quantified over $500 million of leakage in the telecom industry alone.) Provision check, while it can get tricky and frustrating in its implementation, is a simple concept: a company reconciles data from its service systems, its billing systems, and its provisioning systems.

Thus, for a cable company, a provisioning project would compare data from the "headend" management system that tracks activated cable boxes, from the access control system that manages which individual services have been provisioned, and from the billing system that produces invoices. Once the data is manipulated into usable formats, running the comparison produces mounds of exceptions: a not-very-forthcoming Mrs. Johannsen who's been getting cable for free for two years because her account was never entered in the billing system; a Mr. Wilcox who's still, a year later, paying the promotional rate for the package of six movie channels; his next-door neighbor, the nearsighted, trusting Mr. O'Malley, who's been cheerfully paying for HBO for 16 months without ever having actually received it.

Automated revenue maximization tools include software like the provision check tool that detects and analyzes information to discover revenue collection inaccuracies and enables greater confidence in the integrity of revenue collection. They also include preventive tools that work throughout the revenue stream to eliminate sources of revenue leakage.

None of these tools, however, are silver bullets. Companies need process, organizational change, metrics, and leadership to make tools work.

KEY AUTOMATED TOOLS   147

Tools also aren't optional. Because revenue leaks throughout an organization, a truly advanced revenue maximizing company, one committed to achieving major gains in profitability, integrity, and growth from this initiative, will need to examine all of its processes and systems. And it will need to integrate an automated tool on top of almost all systems and *in between* them.

Telecom tools grow up. The telecom industry has seen an explosion of automated revenue maximization tools in the last three years. As recently as 1999, if a company sought an automated tool, it might have had a choice of one or two vendors and tactical advisors with expertise in the general area of the problem. Today, company executives can mischievously put out an RFP, pour themselves a glass of wine, and wait for proposals from six or seven companies that have direct experience in the type of project requested. The vendors will respond with tools that are smarter, more powerful, more functional across a broader spectrum of the revenue cycle, and less expensive than ever before.

Some of the new-tool vendors claim to have built a better mousetrap. Others have repurposed (or even just renamed) existing software to position it as a revenue maximization tool. Others are old-systems vendors that have added revenue maximization functions to their software. (It's unclear sometimes if this functionality is really a new tool. As Gartner Dataquest noted, "A billing, mediation, or churn management product that causes less revenue leakage than another solution does simply what it is designed to do."[1])

A few leading-edge service-sector companies have become savvy at creating their own tools. IT functions, after years as the prom king with little time for buck-toothed, gawky revenue maximization, have begun to realize that revenue maximization is much better looking than they first thought. Vendors are proliferating because tools are becoming more popular. And because tools work. They are wonderful investments, frequently offering a net present value ROI of 10 to 1. (Companies, however, should watch out for desperate vendors promising the moon.)

THE FIVE KEY FEATURES OF AN AUTOMATED TOOL STRATEGY

The five key features of a revenue maximization tool strategy are:

1. **Use of detective tools** to uncover, quantify, and eventually address revenue leakage and inaccuracies in revenue collection
2. **Use of analytical tools** to manage revenue maximization performance and to organize data about and ultimately address recurring sources of leakage
3. **Use of preventive tools** to automate or improve specific processes and eliminate causes of revenue leakage
4. **Constant technological improvement** to leverage the greater power, intelligence, and ease of use of the latest tools
5. **Tools as a living part of company operations**—continuously adjusted, used periodically, and surrounded by processes to capture revenue

As illustrated in Figure 8.1, the first three key features are the use of the distinct types of automated revenue maximization tools. The final two are umbrella strategies to optimize the use of all three types of tools.

FEATURES OF AN AUTOMATED TOOL STRATEGY

Figure 8.1
Key Features of an Automated Tools Strategy

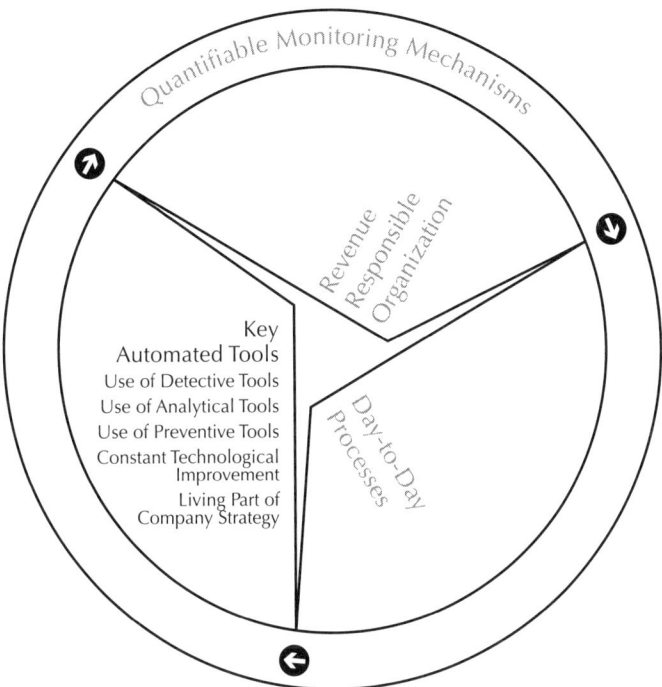

1. Use of detective tools

Sherlock Holmes used a magnifying glass. Today's revenue maximization detectives use sophisticated software tools to uncover and quantify revenue leakage. (Only a few of them, though, smoke pipes or wear deerstalker hats.) Detective tools allow companies to capture revenue immediately by correcting exceptions and to discover root causes of revenue leakage for longer-term preventive strategies. Yet detective tools, as we've said, aren't silver bullets—they may not even be bronze bullets. Their success depends entirely on integrating the tools' information output into rigorous processes to convert that information into revenue capture. As Rich LaPerch of Vibrant Solutions put it, "Technology won't fix management problems, it won't put the right processes in place, and it won't put the right culture in place." Detective tools, however, are the gunpowder of a robust revenue maximization program: they give the program energy, they enable the gun to be fired, and they start the process of fixing revenue leakage. Detective tools, such as the provision check tool, are necessary because of the immense volume of data generated by systems at most companies. Their value, somewhat ironically, lies in their ability to *create new data* from existing systems by isolating individual inaccurate or incomplete transactions, and beginning the process of aggregating data to reveal meaningful patterns.

Detective tools create this data by comparing right and wrong—one system to another with more accurate or complete data, or one system to a purposely constructed ideal. In the last few years, for example, some airlines have built automated "exchange violation" tools to determine when airline ticketing agents in a defined period have exchanged tickets incorrectly—allowing a customer, for example, to swap a $300 ticket for a $900 ticket—and how often violations have occurred in a specific airport or by a specific employee.

Detective tools work by going after the details, the pin-sized holes and inaccuracies in transaction records that add up to major revenue leakage. Sometimes, these detective tools require little computing power as in a "Bill Test" at healthcare companies in which a handful of individual patient records are tracked through company systems to determine, chiefly, the lag time of various payments processes. Yet in most cases, detective tools require major automation. As Chuck Crenshaw, CEO of Connexn Technologies, a software developer for the telecom industry, explained, revenue maximization "entails sifting through lots and lots of records: database records, call detail records, records from multiple sources. It's almost impossible to do on a corporate-wide basis without software tools."

Many industries use dozens of packaged and ad hoc detective tools. The variety of tools and the tactics necessary to apply them deserve a book of their own. We provide two examples below.

Automated billing validation tools. When we railed against checkers checking checkers in the last chapter, we didn't question the goal of checking. A company must actively ensure the accuracy of its billing rates. If a company had only two types of transactions—a shave and a haircut—and two rates—two bits and four bits—this could be done easily. Yet in industries like telecom and healthcare, the spiraling complexity of rates, rate codes, and rate plans, and the occasionally jerry-rigged rate structures strain the ability of manual bill checkers to do an adequate job. Compounding this complexity is the fact that each individual customer may be involved in dozens—or even thousands—of individual transactions (individual telephone calls, for example). Rick Smith of Eschelon stressed how unruly data can become. "We're a medium-sized CLEC," he told us. "And we are billing five or six thousand products. And it's not like you have to get the billing right just once. Those products are always changing because of state and federal regulatory changes and because our own internal marketing group is changing prices up and down all the time."

Enter the computers. The principle behind billing validation tools involves setting up an "independent rating engine" to recalculate a sample set of bills to make sure that the right transaction is being charged the right rate, transaction by transaction, often for millions of records. How does it work? At a local service telecom company, for instance, a type of code is called a USOC—pronounced "you sock"—and represents an individual price for an individual type of service. To set up an independent rating engine, a project team consults the functions responsible for establishing the prices of specific services and constructs an ideal, independent rate table. It then extracts millions of customer records from a company's billing system or, often, multiple billing systems. (Creating the necessary data interfaces can be quite tricky.) The rating engine then multiplies the type of service by the correct USOC, thus producing immaculate bills. The engine then compares the ideal billed prices to the actual billed prices in the billing system and, almost invariably, reveals slews of mispriced monthly recurring charges.

While aggregating these incorrect transactions, the company can detect the causes: random cases of "fat fingers" and mistyped USOCs or, perhaps, whole categories of incorrect USOCs, pointing to interpretation errors between the sales and marketing area and billing areas. A project team at one telecom company frequently had to reach for the aspirin when trying to validate bills for operating units that it had acquired in M&A transactions. "Each market for each product had a unique USOC," the project leader explained to us. "You couldn't understand what you're billing for and whether or not you had the right rates."

The complexity of rates and transaction types grows exponentially when one company resells another company's services—in effect, resells millions of transactions. (Resellers of wireless services are among the most leak-prone segments in the telecom industry, with many leaking 10 to 15 percent of total revenue.) Automated intercarrier billing validation has become a vital part of re-rating and double-checking bills between telecom carriers.

Automated service integrity tools. Many industries have focused attention on using software tools to detect leakage in service-delivery systems. Companies, of course, have a long history of testing, for example, telecom networks and utility grids to see if they work. Using a detective tool to test service integrity from a revenue perspective often requires greater energy and thoroughness. For example, many telecom companies use special automated test call boxes to run periodic tests on their networks to see if calls go through. A revenue maximization project will use these boxes (or variations of them) in a targeted way to test if the duration of calls is being properly recorded for billing purposes.

Test call boxes and similar detective tools produce data not on individual incorrect transactions but on individual network elements that are leaking revenue. An article in *Billing World* reported that one U.S. wireless telecom company, which had earlier cancelled a network testing program because of a lack of resources, resumed the program months later. The company discovered that while its switches worked fine within individual areas, if a wandering customer drove from one area to the next, the company's system didn't catch the call to bill it.[2]

The challenges of detective tools. While, not all detective tool projects are complex, some are. The complexity of these projects often begins with getting the data into usable form. And for all projects, the hardest, most intricate work is converting the data into fixes.

For instance, most companies occasionally do some form of end-to-end reconciliation. This involves following records from one system to the next to make sure nothing falls out before transactions are billed and revenue collected. A smaller telecom company can easily extract 5 million call detail records from two or three of its more straightforward systems that manage different parts of the revenue cycle, compare these records using off-the-shelf database software, and produce exception reports to assist in revenue capture.

Such sunny and bright reconciliation projects do occur, but so do dark and stormy projects. During these types of projects, we remind ourselves that if most data reconciliation were easy, it would already be done. Data challenges can arise from the lack of two sets of data, where comparison is impossible. At electric utilities, for instance, many companies don't have a systematic register of physical locations in a given area. Thus, trying to compare data of all homes or businesses receiving electricity with those actively being metered and billed (by human meter readers) is like clapping with one hand. The opposite problem frequently occurs. A company must clap with fifty hands because it has multiple systems for single processes or multiple sources of data from single systems, such as the AT&T project described earlier that involved 60 different tap points into different systems. Or a revenue maximization team cannot get its hands on available and necessary data, perhaps because the IT function is too busy (or too resistant to the initiative) to provide it.

Tangled and twisted data. Adding to the challenges, the required data is often in an unclear, inconsistent, or odd form, requiring considerable work and aggravating days spent urging—begging, untwisting—data into a format that permits comparison. (These types of projects tend to produce a lot of muttered exclamations of "Automated tools, my foot.") According to a recent survey by our colleagues of 600 executives in all industries in the U.S., U.K., and Australia, nearly 58 percent of all respondents experienced data problems necessitating extra costs to prepare data reconciliations. (Additionally, almost 32 percent of executives said that data quality has led to a failure to bill or collect receivables.)[3]

One company we worked with needed to reconcile data across dozens of provisioning, billing, and intercarrier cost systems. An initial extraction showed that only 20 percent of data matched across the systems. This implied 80 percent leakage, which clearly wasn't the case. As the project team put on its waders and slogged deeper into the swamp, it realized that the circuits sold were recorded under different names in different systems. The network system, for example, listed each individual circuit. The billing system bundled these circuits together if they originated and ended in the same place, recording 200 circuits between, say, Miami and Jacksonville as the "Mia-Jack Circuit Bundle." The provisioning system, however, recorded the same Miami-Jacksonville circuit bundle by another name altogether, such as "February Order." This tangled mess would cause a problem when a customer canceled 20 out of 200 circuits through his or her account representative, who, in turn, would alert the network and billing functions to turn off 20 circuits. The company, however, had no processes in place to adjust the billing for only a portion of the Mia-Jack Circuit Bundle. Some billing clerks handled the situation by canceling the billing of the whole bundle, leading to underbilling. Some clerks couldn't even find the bundle to alter, leading to customers being overbilled and unhappy calls to account reps.

It took weeks of data manipulation to get data into the right format. Yet the work eventually paid off. The project quantified nearly $10 million in revenue in just three months, immediately capturing much of it by using future adjustments and back billing. Over the long term, the company also improved the M&Ps it used to label orders in various systems.

2. USE OF ANALYTICAL TOOLS

Detective tools create new data—individual exceptions, errors, and flaws—and (when they're good) help companies aggregate that data to find patterns. Analytical tools only do the latter, but they are no less essential to a best-practice revenue maximization program. Analytical tools collect, stratify, slice, and dice data to help companies monitor revenue maximization performance, better understand why revenue inaccuracies are happening, and, eventually, convert that information into fixes.

Analytical tools perform tasks that can be as simple—conceptually, if not necessarily technically—as aggregating customer information. For example, with the help of our colleagues, St. Vincent's Catholic Medical Centers in New York implemented a bolt-on application to its patient accounting system to organize and monitor accounts receivable follow-up, significantly improving receivables management. In the telecom industry, BellSouth Cellular (before it became part of the Cingular joint venture) implemented a tool to automate analysis of call records for calls that weren't billed. The tool created detailed reports of rejected calls and provided real-time trending of all types of rejections.[4]

Many companies use tools to analyze customer or payer disputes. We have worked with clients to install analytical tools that categorize disputes periodically—for example, monthly reports of customers complaining of being overbilled for certain services. These systems enable companies

STRATEGY FEATURES: ANALYTICAL TOOLS 157

to analyze the root causes of current leakage and remain vigilant to new proximate causes. They also help them create processes and rules that minimize disputed payments, a major source of untimely and incomplete revenue collection. Similarly, in the healthcare industry, our colleagues have worked with companies to implement powerful denial analysis tools that categorize payment denials by end payer, by service code, by reason for denial, and by other criteria. For years, third-party payer denials were returned in hard copy to healthcare providers and had to be processed (and resubmitted) manually. Payers are now beginning to return denials electronically, allowing the new denial categorization tools to discover which processes demand specific focus and improvement—one group of medical coders, for instance, is fat finger city—or which areas require new processes to handle specific payers' peculiarities.

Real-time monitoring analytical tools are steadily creeping into the telecom, healthcare, and other industries. One telecom company, for instance, has developed its own tool in its billing audit function to allow it, in every billing run, to measure product, customer, and billing metrics. The tool alerts the company if certain aspects of the billing run are notably out of sync with historical data. Other companies (especially in healthcare) have installed variations of the "digital dashboard" concept illustrated in Figure 8.2, in which a company implements a graphically-rich, single-screen monitoring tool to track a dozen or so key revenue-related metrics. (Some call the dashboard a "cockpit," but that seems to imply too many bells and whistles.) In Chapter 10, we detail the importance of analytical tools to a robust monitoring mechanism and to the long-term success of revenue maximization.

Figure 8.2
Sample Revenue Maximization Dashboard

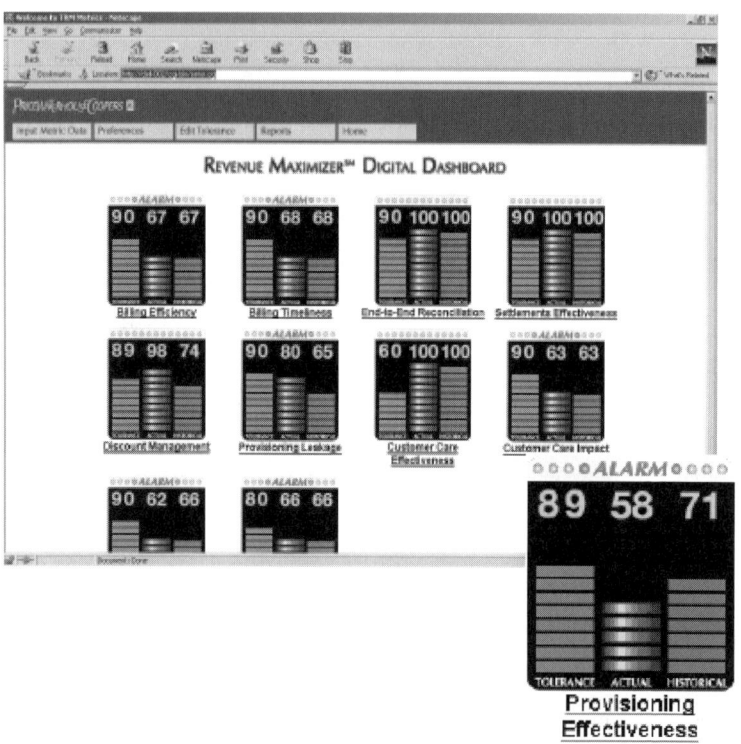

Source: PricewaterhouseCoopers Telecom Revenue Maximizer[SM] Dashboard

3. USE OF PREVENTIVE TOOLS

When most people new to revenue maximization think about tools, their imagination jumps to the supermarket scanner, a tool that automates manual processes and leads a company into a golden valley of leak freedom. Preventive tools are not all as revolutionary as a supermarket scanner, but they are, in their various forms, essential to a best-practice revenue maximization program. Verizon's Karin

Wagar told us, "I'm a proponent of mechanization. Any manual process anywhere in the company is fraught with errors. Companies should put in *as much* mechanization and controls as they can."

Yet companies must keep in mind that many revenue collection-related problems don't lend themselves to preventive tools. Few preventive tools are silver bullets, and fewer still enable "giant leaps." Companies must not use long-term plans to develop them as excuses for short-term plans to do nothing.

Companies must also situate preventive tools in the correct place in a broader revenue maximization program. As a few executives told us, companies can greatly benefit from preventive automation but only *at the end* of a major project. One telecom company we worked with, for example, was able, after process reengineering, to automate 10 of 15 steps of a particular process. Similarly, Web hosting company Interland is beginning to benefit from earnings gains from a major revenue maximization project, which improved customer renewal and customer collection processes. The project redesigned frontline employees' tasks and relationships with the customer. Tools to automate some of these processes came last and were the least of the project's challenges. As Interland's CFO, David Buckel, told us, "You have to change the processes first. Then comes acculturation. Automation comes after. The more you acculturate the change, the more you can automate it."

Preventive tools are currently a motley crew, applicable in varying ways to countless procedures and functions within the revenue cycle. A few representative samples follow.

Inter-system communication tools. Data frequently escapes (and revenue disappears) between systems. This is why many companies have focused on developing tools to make systems better communicate with each other. Some of these tools—electronic data interchange (EDI) of bills with major customers, for example—are now so widespread that they inspire little more than yawns. Many tools are more leading-edge. Certain specialty vendors, for instance, have developed tools that allow normally irascible mainframe systems to get along better. Others are focused on more specific inter-system communication. For instance, a few years ago, Internet service providers (ISPs) suffered notable revenue leakage because the systems that delivered advertising were not integrated with systems to bill advertisers. (Many ISPs would download the ad delivery data into an Excel file and e-mail it to the billing department.) "Middleware" providers have developed tools to eliminate manual steps. Some automated tools insert software and an extra step in particularly error-prone processes. For example, in the healthcare industry, automated "claim-scrubbing" applications identify incomplete or erroneous claims prior to submissions and greatly minimize the manual work that would be needed if claims were rejected by third-party payers.

Autocorrect tools. Many systems eject transaction or order records that they can't process because, for example, of a missing data field. Considerable energy is now going into the development of tools that correct these records automatically, eliminating the need to manually reprocess the records one by one. In the telecom industry, the search for big-picture autocorrection tools has hinged on attempts to find unimpeachable "golden sources" of data to which other systems can be linked and which provide verifiably correct information. For example, a few years ago, many executives hoped that signaling system 7 (SS7) data, which tracks a complete record for every call for network engineering purposes, could be a golden source for billing systems. However, some spectacularly thorny—and to the nonspecialist, spectacularly uninteresting—data challenges have so far slowed this effort. In general, at this point in time, most potential autocorrect tools face problems in finding truly clean sources of data. Rich LaPerch of Vibrant told us, "Right now, it's garbage in, garbage out. How do you develop a rule to decide which garbage is the right garbage?"

Nonetheless, autocorrect tools have been put to work in isolated areas. For example, Jeannette Alberte described a project at one of SBC's units. "Service orders were falling out because our databases were out of sync," Jeannette explained to us. "So we instituted a clean-up initiative. We researched what should be the golden source of data and programmed the database to go to the golden source and automatically update itself." This led to tremendous preventive and efficiency capture: "The project directly translated into a reduction of service orders that had to be manually processed and the amount of service orders that needed intervention to flow through. This resulted in expense savings and improved timeliness of billing customers."

Service optimization tools. Optimizing a network or services can clear up available capacity and prevent inefficiencies from hampering a company's ability to make new sales to willing customers. Many utilities, for example, now use more sophisticated hedging and electricity loading tools to manage capacity and minimize opportunity leakage. Similarly, many airlines have implemented sophisticated yield management software to prevent wasting valuable seats.

British Airways developed its own tool to cancel connecting flights for no-shows on earlier flights, freeing up 400,000 seats a year.[5]

We foresee over the next few years a major expansion of these types of service optimization tools in all industries.

Customer screening tools. Many companies are becoming more sophisticated at installing tools up front to eliminate bad customers who cause leakage wherever by not paying bills or by paying bills late. For example, tools to automate pre-sale credit checks through risk profiling or links to third-party vendors can segment customers, limit a company's risk, and minimize leakage at the uppermost point of the revenue stream.

These same screening tools can occasionally *cause* opportunity leakage. In the Web hosting industry, for instance, our colleagues report that some customer screening tools are too restrictive. Customers denied services for "soft" reasons, like expired credit cards or exceeded credit limits, are lumped together with customers rejected for "hard" reasons, like bad credit or the fact that the customer is using a credit card he just stole in a convenience store robbery.

Manual-process replacement tools. The tools of the popular imagination—tools like supermarket scanners that replace manual processes to prevent revenue leakage and inaccurate revenue collection—do exist in some industries. And they are becoming more important. The healthcare industry, where information processing and charge-capturing processes are often manual and widely distributed across an organization, is constantly (albeit sometimes slowly) searching for and implementing manual-process replacement tools. Some hospitals, for instance, are using mobile computing technology to ensure more charge capture and to prevent leaks that occur because of misinterpreted manual notation of services. Smart card technology that automates patient registration is very slowly being introduced into the U.S. healthcare system. (It is already widespread in France.) Electric, water, and gas utilities are also increasingly adopting technology to replace analog meters prone to causing revenue leakage.

4. Constant technological improvement

A *best-practice* tool strategy demands the use of all three types of tools. It also demands constant improvement by leveraging the best, highest-return, most technologically advanced tools. We aren't suggesting that every company ought to go on a spending spree and buy the fanciest, most expensive tools. For many companies, with shrinking IT budgets and cultural resistance to revenue maximization, buying the most sophisticated tools would be like buying a car before learning how to walk. (And, as we've said, many companies can develop high-return first-generation tools in-house.) Yet, a company that ignores the powerful tools now available and ignores the tool developer's culture of constant improvement and upgrades, will fail to benefit from the greater functionality, ease of use, and flexibility of new tools.

Most automated revenue maximization tools, for example, are simply "getting better" in terms of increased speed and power. For example, according to Gary Ross, Vice President of Product Management and Marketing at Connexn, an average 100,000-circuit line audit used to take

24 hours. Now it takes two minutes.[6] Automated tools are also advancing on several specific fronts:

- **Greater intelligence.** Detective tools both uncover individual cases of revenue leakage and aggregate these cases into patterns that facilitate preventive capture. Many detective tools are improving on the latter function, automating pattern recognition and making revenue capture easier. Chuck Crenshaw of Connexn told us that, in the telecom industry, "in the near-term, the software's built-in industry intelligence—the rules-based intelligence—is going to improve and allow for the outcome of the detection process to be reported in a much more usable and real-time fashion. Today, companies without automated tools mostly get a formatted dump of information, have to do a lot of 'stare and compare,' and are forced to do a real significant intellectual exercise to see what they can do to fix a problem."

- **Minimally intrusive.** In some industries, revenue maximization tools weren't historically feasible because they intruded on a company's systems and ongoing operations. For instance, in the airline industry, running a detective tool used to be difficult because ticketing databases were sensitive and could rarely be tapped for external analysis. Yet now, more powerful computers can scan and extract data more quickly, allowing the use of exchange violation revenue maximization tools.

- **Web-based.** Much of the value of revenue maximization tools—analytical tools in particular—comes from their being accessible to (and actually looked at by) a wide group of executives and managers within a company. Web-based, sequel server environments are ideal for these tools, allowing for a broader access to data. Web technologies also provide more graphically appealing tools and easier manipulation of data.

5. Tools as a living part of company operations

We once wrote that tools are like heart bypass surgery: a discrete operation happens but a change in lifestyle is necessary for success. We were accused of being grim at the time—one wise guy still makes heart jokes when he sees us—but a lifestyle change is necessary, in two ways. First, to maximize revenue, to eliminate inaccuracies in revenue collection, a company must integrate tools into robust, proactive processes to fix proximate causes of those inaccuracies. Second, a company must develop processes to periodically reapply and update detective and analytical tools.

Fix causes or accomplish little. A tool strategy, like a fire prevention strategy, aims for sharply diminishing returns. Every city in the world would love to have a fire department that has nothing to do all day except make itself chili and get cats out of trees. Every robust revenue maximizer hopes that someday its detective tools find not a penny in leaked (or inaccurate) revenue. But to begin to see diminishing returns requires wrapping tools into broader processes for immediate and preventive revenue capture. In fact, analytical and detective tools only have value inside these broader processes. *If a company doesn't implement tools with the right energy, resources, people, and processes to execute fixes, it's probably not worth implementing them at all.*

It's easy to understand why preventive capture demands will and energy. Root causes of revenue leakage take time to correct, especially if they demand changing long-standing day-to-day processes or retraining key frontline employees. Isolating root causes of leakage for preventive capture often requires considerable and time-consuming massaging of data produced by detective tools.

Immediate revenue capture also takes time and requires manual intervention. In the telecom industry, for instance, a detective tool can identify tens of thousands of exceptions—records, for instance, of a service or call delivered but not billed. Companies need first to validate that these exceptions represent actual leakage and weren't produced, for example, because the definition of leakage was too broad. Some of this validation can be done by linking data back to original system sources, but some needs to be performed manually.

Once exceptions are validated, immediate capture can still demand significant manual work. For instance, if a provisioning tool applied at a cable company reveals that 10,000 customers are receiving free or wrongly-priced services, a clerk must often alter customer records by hand. (Immediate capture can get *really* tricky when complicated business-to-business contracts and rate structures are involved.) Tools can produce so much manual immediate-capture work that some companies have chosen to manage the post-detection process carefully. One telecom company we worked with decided to release to its clerks only 200 corrections at a time. If they hadn't done this, some employees would have come whistling in to work one morning and have seen a "things to do" list containing thousands of fixes, which is the type of morning greeting most of us could do without.

Similarly, new preventive tools frequently demand advanced technical skills, and the potential benefits of these tools is limited if a company's staff can't use them right. As Alexander Cibenko of Saint Vincent Catholic Medical Centers of New York said to us, "A lot of the functionality of the new client server applications is dependent upon the end user being able to manipulate the technology. You need to have advanced skills in your IT staff and the individual operational departments running new bolt-on technology or you're not going to be able to grab hold of the benefits." Alex explained that he is sometimes hesitant to bring in new, leak-prevention technology: "Unless new technology products and services are a fit, are easy to use, and I can integrate them with my skill levels of my staff, I just have fears that the effort to manage the technology will be greater than the benefits of the newly-proposed systems, that they will suck up our time and resources and distract us from our primary focus to expeditiously process patients and collect cash."

Some companies accomplish little. As commonsensical as the above advice may seem, we are surprised that many companies still don't fix leakage by wrapping revenue maximization tools into programs. This occasionally may be justified—when, for example, the ROI of fixing root causes doesn't surpass a necessary hurdle. But often, companies don't address root causes because of the susceptibilities we talked about in Chapter 3. One telecom company we know of used a detective tool on an admirably periodic basis. It found about 5 million call records that fell out of its system on an admirably periodic basis. Yet it patted itself on the back on an admirably periodic basis as long as this number didn't increase. The company made no attempt to determine if a simple investment (or a simple process change or business rule) could reduce this number even to 4 million calls.

Another telecom company, a small CLEC, went after the exceptions with all the urgency of a turtle crossing a beach. A detective tool had produced thousands of exceptions. It took the company's project team over 15 months to work through them, transaction by transaction, for immediate revenue capture. *After* that, the company started to think about addressing root causes even though the leaks from 15 months ago were no longer relevant to the proximate causes that the company was then experiencing.

Analytical tools, too, are often used improperly. One company we worked with implemented a sophisticated analytical monitoring tool that generated high-level metrics on a monthly basis for key executives. The company had even established a monthly revenue maximization meeting. This provided a nice opportunity for various executives to sit around a table, drink fresh coffee, nibble on pastries, and blame other functions for causing revenue leakage.

Plug and leave doesn't work. Living tools are actively managed, continuously adjusted for new systems and products and, most important, utilized periodically. Companies should be able to run—and should run—automated tools again and again with little fuss, little outside help, and little incremental investment.

Yet, we have frequently seen companies use tools diagnostically, solely to achieve peace of mind. They assess billing systems, correct rate table errors, and then move on to "more important things." This approach would work fine if a company planned never to install a new system, launch a new product, or change a single price. But new leaks can originate overnight. When, for example, new systems are installed, a company must design and perform a new process for end-to-end reconciliation to ensure that new transactions don't leak through newly-formed joints.

And even if a company decided never to change its business, it would also have to dictate a corporate policy that no one could ever make a mistake again. In the airline industry where much leakage is caused by human error or bad judgment, the quarterly or annual running of certain detective tools is necessary to closely watch for newly-appearing leakage patterns.

The biggest objection to reusing tools periodically is that the cost would bust the budget. Yet tools not only aim for diminishing returns, they also benefit from diminishing costs. Much of the work in implementing automated tools involves the upfront customization of a tool to a company's systems. Tools already customized with the right interfaces and right business rules built in often demand little in incremental investment other than people's time to run them and some further alteration when systems change. Companies, however, must be cautious not to customize tools to a point of undue complication. "The biggest obstacle our customers face," explained Rich LaPerch of Vibrant, "is that the more customization that is required, the less likely that tools will be used long term. So, in many organizations, tools are not used to their full potential."

Telecom CLEC Eschelon has used tools to their full potential. For instance, it developed a tool to reconcile its customer billing to what other carriers were billing. The tool became a living, value-creating part of the company. "I had always thought that we were doing reconciliations," Eschelon's President Rick Smith told us. "We weren't really doing reconciliations. We were doing, at best, spot checks on databases. We didn't have a mechanized tool to compare 130,000 lines we were billing versus the 130,000 lines we were being billed for." One system generated the bills and another system managed costs; both systems had to capture the same time, connection, and disconnection data of each call going through the circuits. The detective tool enabled Eschelon to do this. "The tool allowed us savings of $1 million per year. We're now into our second year, so that's $2 million for an investment that was a fraction of that." Most important, Rick concluded, "I have a group of people who now understand the tool, who do it on a regular basis. I'd do a project like that all day long. It was relatively simple. It has a wonderful cost-benefit associated with it. And it increased the competency of our people."

The "end state" of automated tools involves organizational change and new robust processes to make tools a permanent, living part of a company's operations. Revenue maximization software tools combat inaccuracies everywhere—on top of various operating systems at a company and *in between* them. Real-time analytical tools constantly alert companies to areas of acute leakage. Detective tools periodically identify leaking transactions and further uncover root causes and patterns. Dedicated teams and best-practice procedures address the causes immediately. And for particularly intractable root causes, companies implement preventive tools to automate the process.

Actions a company can take now

1. **Listen to the pitches and learn as much as you can.** It's important for a beginner company to understand broadly, at the outset of a revenue maximization initiative, what automated tools are available and in what direction tools in its industry are heading. This means going to conferences and listening to individual tool vendors and consultants—a relatively painless process that often includes free lunch.

2. **Perform a pilot project.** All first-time revenue maximization tool projects at a company will be, by definition, pilot projects. We recommend very "piloty" pilot projects in which a company initially uses detective tools on a small *sample* of transactions within a single area. AT&T's Ellyce Brenner, a zealous proponent of automation, strongly advocates this. "We would not have gotten funding," she told us, "if we were not able to show rigor of sampling and testing. I would encourage executives to pick areas and do the kind of sampling work we've done."

   In contrast, we have seen companies trying to eat a four-foot hoagie of a tool project in one sitting without the organizational commitment necessary for success. These projects have often failed as dreams of a silver bullet faded and enthusiasm withered.

   Managing success and starting small are particularly important to ensure cross-functional buy-in of automated tool projects. Aggregating and comparing information across the revenue stream is integral to many detective and analytical tools. If people within functions throughout the stream don't believe in the project, they will rarely be eager to provide the necessary data or to follow through on the steps necessary for revenue capture.

3. **Do something that's been done before.** In revenue maximization, if not in writing, clichés are good. In many industries, vendors and outside advisors have performed particular types of projects repeatedly. The basics of these projects are well known. For example, in many industries, end-to-end reconciliation makes for a good initial project. The value of a database reconciliation is usually understood by the organization, and a company can usually complete more clear-cut reconciliation projects in two or three months.

Even better, beginner companies should, if possible, do something *their own* company has done before. Verizon, for example, often repeats projects. As Karin Wagar explained, "The easiest thing to do is to take tools that we had already used and propagate them in other territories. We've found incredible payback in that. Number one, it brings a revenue lift because we're going after the easiest low-hanging fruit. Number two, it gets us good press and good exposure within the company."

4. **Develop processes.** Companies should build formal, best-practice M&Ps around converting tool-generated data into captured revenue on a regular and consistent basis.

5. **Integrate detective and analytical tools into a master dashboard.** As we discuss in Chapter 10, best-practice quantifiable monitoring mechanisms demand a sim-

plified, integrated, and tiered approach that involves regular application of key tools in a master metrics program.

6. **Develop skills.** As companies advance in revenue maximization, they should bring basic tool expertise in-house, especially knowledge needed to reapply detective tools periodically.
7. **Lead the industry.** Experienced revenue maximization companies should be on the leading edge of all tools, particularly preventive tools, not only in acquiring them from vendors and outside advisors but helping to develop them and customize them to the companies' particular revenue leakage issues.

Notes

1. Scholz, "Revenue Assurance Services Providers," 1.

2. Michelle Hankins, "Revenue Assurance at the Switch," *Billing World*, (January 2001).

3. PricewaterhouseCoopers, *Global Data Management Survey 2001* (New York: PricewaterhouseCoopers, 2002), 2.

4. Michelle Hankins, "Wireless Revenue Assurance," *Billing World*, (November 2000).

5. Feldman, "Out of the Window," 49.

6. Susan McNeice, "Data Reconciliation: Service Provider Salvation, or Just a Back-Office Bandage," *Billing World*, (March 2002).

Chapter Nine

The Revenue Responsible Organization

With revenue maximization, if a company organizes, motivates, and provides incentives to people to maximize revenue because it's worthwhile, because it adds value, and because it's the right thing to do, *things will get done.* Leadership is essential. People drive tools and process and metrics projects, and, from day one, a company must lay a cultural, organizational, and attitudinal foundation if it wants to accomplish anything. This chapter, in part, discusses what's needed from the first day.

The focus of this chapter, however, is creating the end goal, **the revenue responsible organization**, in which ownership of and enthusiasm for revenue maximization exists throughout the company, in which the strategy is considered mission critical to the strengthening of profitability, integrity, and growth, and in which a core revenue maximization function is the revenue *conscience* of the organization. Tolerance is, of course, a wonderful thing, but a true revenue responsible organization is a blessedly intolerant one—intolerant of a penny of revenue leakage.

The revenue responsible organization is the end goal, but it's also the journey to get there. And so this chapter focuses on the specific features of a revenue responsible organization that ensure the cultural and organizational commitment necessary for success. Broadly speaking, all the features help a company extend the commitment of early champions—the core team managing the initiative, the team embracing the success factors discussed in Chapter 4—to the larger organization.

But organizational change is not the first step. The momentum to change the organization, the force necessary to crash through the wall of habit, must be earned with success. And frankly, major organizational change is not necessary at every company. If a company wants to pick up a couple of million dollars in revenue a year, it doesn't need to worry about a formal revenue maximization function. (That is, unless the company's revenue is only a couple of million dollars a year.) If, however, a company wants to actually maximize revenue, to capture all the revenue and only the revenue it deserves from the services it has already provided, it needs to create a revenue responsible organization.

This will often evolve naturally if success is managed and achieved. At one recent project, which began under a cloud of skepticism and begrudging participation, we saw excitement palpably grow, almost on a week-by-week basis. The team members gradually began to consider, louder and more concretely, the organizational change necessary to bottle the lightning of its first projects.

The six key features of a revenue responsible organization

We were tempted to be tough and curt when laying out a best-practice revenue responsible organization by simply quoting Jack Welch when he wrote, "Giving the project visibility, putting great people on it, and giving them plenty of money continues to be the best formula for success."[1] Really, that's all you need. In the end, though, we decided to be careful and methodical and lay out the key features necessary to create a revenue responsible organization. As Figure 9.1 illustrates, there are six key features:

1. **Executive support and leadership** from top executives, dedicated revenue maximization executives, and functional executives
2. **Measured participation of *all* levels of management,** with a particular focus on ensuring middle-management cooperation
3. **Resources**—skilled people and money
4. **A formal revenue maximization function** to both conduct revenue maximization projects and guide the organization
5. **Collaborative participation of the whole revenue cycle,** achieved through both formal and informal thrusts to combat the silo mentality
6. **Continuous improvement and tangible change,** with real, newly acquired skills improving a company's ability to maximize revenue

Figure 9.1
Key Features of a Revenue Responsible Organization

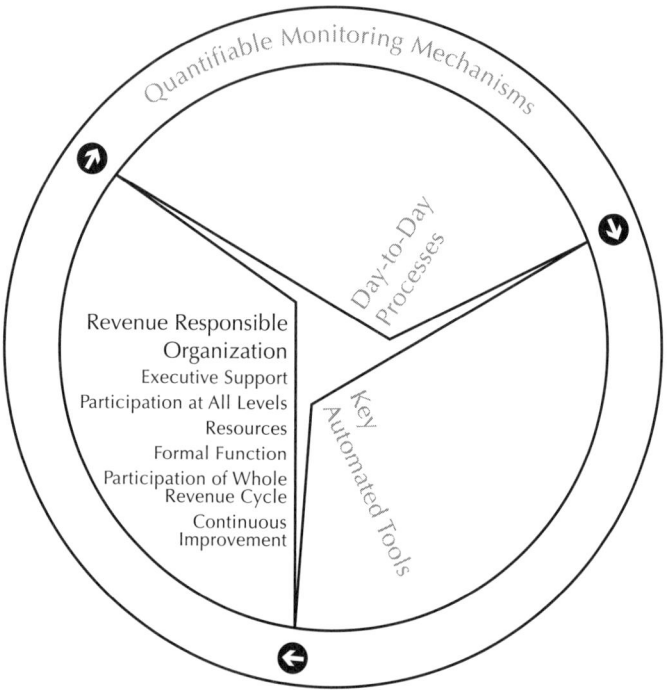

1. Executive support and leadership

Back in the "olden" days of our practice—about 1998—we tended to list the more tangible features of the revenue responsible organization first: resources or incentives for middle managers. The research for this book, however, convinced us that although we thought that executive support was really important, we still underestimated its significance. So often at companies, once an initiative gains executive support, all the other features we discuss in this chapter—collaboration, middle-management participation, resources—fall into line.

Without some form of *all three* kinds of executive support—top executive support, dedicated executive support, and functional executive support—companies will sputter along, accomplishing little. Circumstances still force too many companies into this situation. As Pete Varley of Bell Canada put it, "They have a solution without an owner."

Top executive support. Support for revenue maximization by corporate or divisional CEOs is often evident in a vague sort of way. As one executive told us, "Our CEO doesn't necessarily fully understand it, but he has the notion that he has people who understand revenue assurance and are doing something about it." While this vague support is nice (and prevalent, probably, because it's not too hard too vaguely support anything), another type of top executive support—tangible, steadfast, incessant—can be extraordinarily powerful.

In the last decade, the companies accomplishing the most with revenue maximization, cost reduction, or any corporate efficiency initiative have been the ones in which top executives drive the initiatives, direct people to succeed, make them accountable for doing it, and ensure that managers and frontline employees believe that the goal is important, value-added, and exciting. Executive leadership *in and of itself* can sometimes produce benefits. One large company we worked with had assembled a portfolio of international wireless telecom assets with varying and, in a few cases, unacceptable levels of revenue leakage. The parent company systematically communicated the importance of revenue maximization to the top executives at each portfolio company. These executives, without significant resources but with energy and imagination, created focus, developed plans, and carried through on well-designed strategies. Many of the companies quantified 2 to 10 percent in revenue leakage and captured significant incremental revenue growth.

Lessons from Canada. Bell Canada is indicative of what can happen with executive leadership and support. As Pete Varley told us, "Although we started small with a consumer market initiative, the program had full executive sponsorship. This enabled us to manage it aggressively, and with a revenue-growth mindset, not an audit mindset." Mike McGrath, who's part of the leadership team at the pioneering Bell Ontario business unit, went even further in his explanation of the unit's success: "The most significant tactical enabler of our success is our leadership approach." The top leader of Bell Ontario, Terry Mosey, fully praises the hard blocking and tackling of the frontline revenue maximization teams, but, he doesn't downplay his own role. "Revenue assurance takes leadership at the most senior part of the business," he stressed. "It takes the same intensity and focus that we apply to other things where leadership makes a difference."

What precisely does leadership do? First, it brings attention to revenue maximization. "To me," Terry explained, "it comes down to corporate priorities. Everyone has his or her top five priorities, and it requires a lot of influence and persuasion to get a project up the list. It's not just a matter of silos, it's a matter of attention." Next, as Terry also explained, "Leadership creates passion and intensity." This passion and intensity create a "please the boss" momentum, in which employees, managers, and executives all self-motivatedly pursue revenue maximization. Karin Wagar of Verizon made a revenue maximization pilgrimage with other telecom executives to Bell Canada. Karin later related to us,

"I was very impressed by the creativity there, by how they got the employees—the grass roots—to bubble up opportunities."

Finally, the revenue maximization champions at Bell Canada understand and can penetrate the social architecture of the organization. They use informal persuasion to challenge the resistant and to inspire everyone to pursue the profitability, integrity, and growth opportunities within the company.

Dedicated revenue maximization executive support. Some also benefit from a second crucial type of executive support: a dedicated revenue maximization executive. A revenue maximization "czar" is vitally important as both a symbol and an engine. A newly-appointed czar who's sufficiently high in the organization can accelerate attention simply by being appointed to the role, signaling that management takes revenue maximization seriously. Sometimes, if the appointment is high enough, it can be a kind of shock therapy. ("Sally Smith has been appointed *what?*") In the healthcare industry, denial management is a crucial issue. According to Alex Cibenko of St. Vincent's Health Systems, "It's not uncommon in a market where managed care has good penetration to see 6, 7, or 8 percent of claims denied." To handle this problem, a few organizations have put individuals whose sole responsibility is payment denials in the *top* executive suite. A revenue maximization czar is not simply a symbol. His or her leadership is necessary to get things done. One of the reasons we recommend a highly-placed dedicated executive is that he or she should have enough institutional weight to be a silo breaker, to get functions to work together, and to push a resistant organization ahead with an unyielding bias for action. Some dedicated executives can do this even without day-to-day top-executive support. Jeannette Alberte of SBC argued to us that there are only two paths to success: "You have to have executive sponsorship and have someone willing to go to bat for you. Or you have to put on blinders and barrel ahead."

Finally, a highly-respected executive is more likely to lead an effective formal revenue maximization function.

Other functional executive support. Support needs to be broadly distributed throughout an organization, specifically among the executives in charge of the silos (IT, customer care, sales and marketing, etc.) necessary for cross-functional collaboration. For large companies, we recommend setting up an executive steering committee—similar to the "productivity councils" at many companies—to develop ongoing operational objectives for revenue maximization, to help prioritize action plans, and most importantly, to ensure that each function views revenue maximization as essential to corporate success and to the function's own mission.

Broad executive support is less essential atop different business units. In our experience, business units can pursue revenue maximization at their own pace without disrupting the company's overall efforts. Laggard divisions generally catch up when they understand the opportunity.

2. MEASURED PARTICIPATION OF ALL LEVELS OF MANAGEMENT

As sad as a tale of a revenue maximization initiative without executive support can be, equally sad is an initiative without middle-management support. In our discussions with executives and observers across industries, we were reminded anew that measured participation at *all* levels of management is essential to becoming a revenue responsible organization.

One executive we spoke to relayed her frustrating experience with resistant middle management: "When management at the middle level got instructions from the higher level, they found a way to convince senior management that the opportunity was smaller and that the only way to capture revenue would be to invest in major systems changes that were really expensive. They managed to convince upper management to step back from the program." This is not an isolated experience. One technology-company executive told us, "One area that hasn't been a problem has been executive recognition of the opportunity. The problems are more cultural—many of our people are resisting change." At one large telecom company, the CEO communicated to his direct reports his desire to seize revenue maximization opportunities enterprisewide. This, alas, didn't spark a vigorous program. His direct reports assigned the task of establishing a strategy to specific managers. These resistant, defensive managers sat upon the initiative until they squeezed the last bit of life out of it. (Now, a few years later, the company has experienced tremendous success with and enthusiasm for revenue maximization in a few isolated areas.)

When we attend early, high-level discussions of revenue maximization, four of five companies insist they are "doing revenue assurance." Yet, in 99 out of 100 cases, the companies aren't really doing anything. Senior executives too often confuse setting strategy on revenue maximization with executing it. And they are frequently not executing because the middle managers responsible for the actual execution are, for a variety of reasons, not pursuing revenue maximization projects with the minimum energy to quantify and capture leaked revenue.

So, measure it. Creating participation at all levels of management requires measuring participation. Companies who treat revenue maximization seriously will have compensation and personal targets for managers and executives based, to some extent, on revenue maximization goals. We have started, for example, to see some telecom companies holding managers and executives accountable, if only by including revenue maximization as part of an overall revenue growth target. (We have not seen any company, though, reach the type of commitment that GE devoted to Six Sigma in tying 40 percent of its variable compensation to Six Sigma-related criteria.[2]) While most executives and managers rank being subject to new revenue maximization compensation-criteria the same as being attacked by killer bees—people don't like being held accountable for new, unfamiliar initiatives—we believe, in the long term, such criteria are necessary to create a revenue responsible organization. Revenue responsible organizations shouldn't stimulate participation solely by fear, of course. As a colleague of ours notes, healthcare companies that are successfully maximizing revenue find, "a sugar cube has been better than a hammer." Companies should create incentives to motivate managers to increase profitability rather than disincentives tied to revenue collection inaccuracies.

3. Resources

Resources—a catch-all phrase for people and money—are a basic ingredient of revenue maximization success. Unfortunately, acquiring resources for the initiative has never been more difficult than now, precisely when companies need the benefits of the initiative more than ever. Over the last several years, we have surveyed both cable and telecom executives who, overwhelmingly, cited lack of resources—both hard skills and money—as top barriers to maximizing revenue.

Resources are needed to acquire tools and to obtain help from external advisors and vendors. But resources are also needed for basic blocking and tackling—the manual tasks necessary for immediate revenue capture, such as changing rate tables, altering particular contract stipulations, or entering correct data into provisioning systems. One telecom company needed clerks for a revenue capture project and couldn't find available people within the organization. It decided, in the end, to hire back people recently laid off on a temporary basis.

Best-practice revenue responsible organizations need more than clerks. They need skilled resources, including experts (or potential experts) in data manipulation, metrics design, and process improvement. They also need people with specific technical knowledge in complicated products and billing and contract terms. Of course, revenue maximization initiatives need people with IT skills not only to help develop tools but to understand a company's systems for all types of projects. And revenue maximization demands people with softer skills, such as the ability to motivate others and work with other functions.

One way companies can develop some of the harder skills is by intelligently integrating their program teams with skilled outside advisors who are conducting various revenue maximization projects and making knowledge transfer an explicit goal of these projects.

Where are the resources? We offer three pieces of advice to revenue maximization champions struggling for resources:

- **Be creative.** Especially in the early resistant phases of the path to commitment, getting resources (money in particular) for revenue maximization can be like squeezing blood from a stone. Yet relentless leaders, magicians all, manage to do it. One revenue maximization executive told us how he was forced, as the saying goes, to "beg, borrow, and steal" in the startup phase of the initiative.
- **Reallocate resources.** We've repeatedly mentioned efficiency capture opportunities from revenue maximization, and we strongly recommend that some of this "captured efficiency" be reallocated to revenue maximization projects. Many companies have the right *number* of people to get the job done. They are simply using them for lower-return projects and tasks.
- **Make revenue maximization self-funding.** One of the greatest guarantors of sufficient revenue maximization resources is to make the initiative self-funding. In the broadest sense, revenue maximization is almost always self funding: revenue generated exceeds investment. (If it didn't, then this book should be titled *Revenue Maximization: A Colossal Waste of Time.*) Yet an explicitly self-funding initiative has mechanisms in place so that the budgeting process formally treats revenue maximization costs as the direct reinvestment of revenue maximization wins.

Finally, a company's perception of revenue maximization can determine the resources it dedicates to the initiative. At leading revenue maximization companies, executives straightforwardly and impartially compare revenue maximization against other revenue growth initiatives. It is seen as a critical part of the organization's strategy for profitability, integrity, and growth. If revenue maximization never receives all the funding its champions hope for, they still go to bed knowing that the initiative was treated on a more or less equal footing with other opportunities. In most cases, initiatives rarely received all of the funding their champions wanted either.

4. A FORMAL REVENUE MAXIMIZATION FUNCTION

From the first day of a revenue maximization initiative, a company does not need a formal, chartered, staffed, and resourced revenue maximization function. Yet a lingering ad hoc approach—a task force maybe, or "borrowed" staff—will stymie efforts to maximize revenue in the long term. The strategy cannot be another responsibility added to someone's already burdensome workload. Stamp collecting is a good hobby, gardening is a good hobby, but revenue maximization is a horrible hobby. It must be a job.

In smaller organizations, a formal revenue maximization team can do most of the heavy lifting of managing and staffing individual revenue maximization projects. In larger organizations, in which business units or individual functions often provide the resources for the heavy lifting, a formal function can serve as the brains, the rocket packs, and the *guide* dogs—not just auditing watchdogs—of all revenue maximization activities.

The benefits of a formal function. Ellyce Brenner of AT&T captured the benefits of a formal function when she argued that a company needs a central robust revenue maximization team so that "you don't miss learning across the board, so that you can leverage components of the program, so that you're not always reinventing the wheel, so that you have some consistency across the product streams, and so that you have a key body of knowledge that you keep on improving." In our experience, a formal function:

- Ensures dedicated management and skilled technical resources
- Is minimally intrusive by not taking core revenue maximization resources away from other tasks
- Spreads enthusiasm and commitment to revenue maximization by working the organization
- Enables the faster completion of projects by leveraging past successes and understanding of best practices
- Achieves economies of scale and *preserves resources* by enabling the efficient repetition of projects in multiple areas of a company; Verizon, as we said, took a tool built for one unit and "propagated" it in other units
- Promotes increased accountability enterprisewide for revenue maximization tasks and metrics by preventing revenue maximization responsibility from being too thinly distributed across self-interested functions
- Builds corporate knowledge

The final benefit is perhaps the most important. Formal function team members are the thought leaders. They attend conferences. They must develop real expertise, or frankly, people won't rely on them.

Table 9.1 lists potential team members of a formal revenue maximization function.

Table 9.1
Potential Core Members of Formal Revenue Maximization Function

Title	Responsibilities/Characteristics
Revenue Maximization Executive	Work with senior management. Champion, oversee, and direct revenue maximization effort.
Director of Operations	Manage day-to-day implementation of all projects, including tool implementation. (At larger companies, operations function may be handled by a team with specialists in contract management, data analysis, business rules, and technology.)
Manager of Change Management	Ensure revenue maximization in all change and proactively involved in revenue maximization implications of any new revenue impacting event, including new products, acquisitions, and technology.
Manager of Performance Measurement	Develop, monitor, and analyze Key Performance Indicators.
Manager of Continuous Improvement and Special Projects	Improve and streamline revenue maximization tools, processes, and procedures and contribute to facilitate special projects.
Manager of Fraud Prevention	Manage all anti-fraud activities. (If anti-fraud activities are outside revenue maximization, they should be brought into core team.)
Subject Matter Expert	Contribute expertise for complicated technologies or product types (e.g., intercarrier billing or wireless data in the telecom industry).

Creating a formal function. A formal function varies according to company size and depends on wider organizational decisions. We offer two general pieces of advice on creating a function. First, the people in the function must be what Jack Welch and others call A players, not B or C players, or the function, given the relentlessness, leadership, and creativity required, won't succeed. (At GE, Six Sigma "Black

Belt" training is given only to A players. Also, some years, at certain management levels, only A players with Six Sigma training received stock option grants.[3]) Second, a function should be built from the ground up. Our team has worked with companies on revenue responsible organization projects, which systematically review a company's organization, outline all the probable tactical projects for the next two or three years, determine the skills and employees necessary for those projects, decide whether these skills should be located in the formal function, outside the function, or outside the company, and begin a methodical process to assemble the function's team.

5. Collaborative participation of the whole revenue cycle

Revenue maximization is hampered by the silo mentality, and revenue leakage is caused by it. A revenue responsible organization must, therefore, create an organization and culture that promotes cross-functional collaboration and communication. In our earliest writings about revenue maximization, we underestimated how hard ensuring collaborative participation would be. We have since collected "silo stories" with a morbid enthusiasm second only to our collection of "big leakage stories." For example, one telecom executive shared us with his frustration trying to get the IT function to put an edit into a provisioning system that would prevent significant revenue leakage: "We went to IT and said, 'We're losing this much money because we don't have an edit in the system.' They said, 'Go train your customer care people.' But we could have trained them till the cows come home and we would still have needed the edit in the system."

Needless to say, creating cross-functional collaboration is a larger issue than creating it for the purpose of revenue maximization—companies strive everyday in every goal to create what Jack Welch calls "boundaryless behavior." (Attempts to do this occasionally move into the cute and the wacky—the corporate Kumbaya retreats, the corporate coin-collector clubs and dog-lover clubs, the "village squares" resembling knock-off Parisian coffee houses plopped down into a range of cubicles.) In our experience, creating collaborative participation to maximize revenue demands formal and informal thrusts.

Formal thrusts. Formal thrusts involve building M&Ps and measured processes to further collaboration. In its inspiring process redesign initiative, Henry Ford Health Systems created team manager positions in each specialty. These managers linked essential revenue-cycle functions like charge-capture staff, medical record coders, trainers, and billers. The managers also had responsibility to advise and consult the individual specialty's physician and administrative management on revenue cycle issues. Formal collaborative thrusts also include writing accountability and measurability goals and procedures for revenue maximization into all corporate functions whose participation is needed.

Informal thrusts: talking the talk. Just as important, revenue maximization leaders must work informally to promote cross-functional participation. For example, leaders of revenue maximization projects ought to have basic project management skills to ensure that the projects run smoothly between functions. More importantly, initiative leaders should be able to somehow *change attitudes* to revenue maximization from naturally resistant functional units. Terry

Mosey phrased this attitudinal change as putting "a new software load in their heads." At Bell Canada, Terry noted, "We were able to change the language at meetings in functional areas. We were able to hit lightbulbs when we shared with them the opportunities."

Executives we spoke to stressed that it's incumbent upon early champions of revenue maximization to *sell* the initiative. For one, they can better sell and inspire collaboration by speaking to functions in their own language. Pat Walker of Qwest told us, "I think the mistake that some revenue assurance people make is that they try to sell revenue assurance for revenue assurance's sake. If I talk to network operations, I make sure to position it as revenue assurance for network's sake."

The single most powerful tool for ensuring collaboration is something we stress in every chapter of this book: *success.* Success is how a revenue maximization initiative produces the champions and evangelists within individual functions. We have seen, time and again, normally hostile functions—hostile in a cold war sort of way—become old buddies once a project delivers great returns and once praise is shared. On one of our first projects, we did an enterprisewide diagnostic on an international telecom company. When we presented the results, hostility filled the room: eyes narrowed in blame at others for causing the leakage. The only seed of a collaborative spirit was an additional, universal hostility directed at us. No function wanted to be part of the project, but the project continued because top management insisted on it. But as the successes began, as momentum built, executives and managers began to contribute and cooperate more to accelerate the momentum further.

They even ended up liking us.

6. Continuous improvement and tangible change

It should be clear by now that revenue maximization is not a one-time effort to diagnose and fix a few cases of incomplete or inaccurate revenue collection. Best-practice revenue responsible organizations not only continually focus on capturing leaked revenue but also continually improve how they do it. Leading revenue responsible organizations strive to maximize revenue increasingly faster, with fewer people, and with more automation.

A best-practice company will not just declare revenue maximization a priority; it will change the organization to achieve it. It will gradually weave tangible skills into the organization—skills, for example, in operating automated tools, in reengineering day-to-day processes, in converting tool data into revenue capture, and in designing and integrating metrics. With each project, with each advance, these tangible skills are added to corporate intelligence. Revenue maximization becomes a core competency.

What's the best organizational structure?

The six core features—with the important exception of a formal revenue maximization function—are more about ends than means. All describe features of a best-practice revenue responsible organization without describing actual paths of responsibility and formal organizational structure. The reason for this is simple: we're more interested in the ends than the means. More to the point, an organizational structure, like a haircut, is a personal issue. Most companies should choose an organization best suited to their idiosyncrasies.

Nevertheless, a debate has erupted in industries about the best organizational structure. (This debate gives us a lot of pleasure. It means that people are becoming passionate enough about revenue maximization to argue about it.) The debate isn't about the need for a formal function. All executives we spoke to insisted that a formal function was a minimum requirement for a revenue responsible organization. (The executives without a robust function strongly wished for one.) The debate also isn't about the end goal. Irrespective of their own success, all the executives agreed that a revenue maximization structure needs to ensure cooperation of executives and managers in three corporate groups—the revenue maximization function, P&L owners, and functional units.

Rather, the debate is about who owns revenue maximization and who drives responsibility forward. As Figure 9.2 illustrates, three basic models exist: the direct model, the finance matrix model, and the operations matrix model. Choosing one should not dominate the agenda on the first day of a revenue maximization initiative. Yet the choice will, inevitably, need to be made at companies fully committed to capturing all the revenue and only the revenue they deserve.

THE DIRECT MODEL

Perhaps the most effective revenue maximization model is the simplest and most direct one: make the revenue maximization leader a cabinet-level post reporting directly to the CEO or, depending on the company, to the COO along with other functional executives (the head of sales, head of IT, etc). This model's advantages are many. The "steering committee" that ensures functional buy-in of revenue maximization is the executive committee that manages the whole company. No separation exists between P&L owners and revenue maximization because revenue maximization sits directly under the top executives responsible for the whole enterprise. Also, the power of the initiative is magnified by the leader's position, not only as a revenue maximization czar but as a senior executive of the company.

Figure 9.2
Three Revenue Maximization Organizational Models

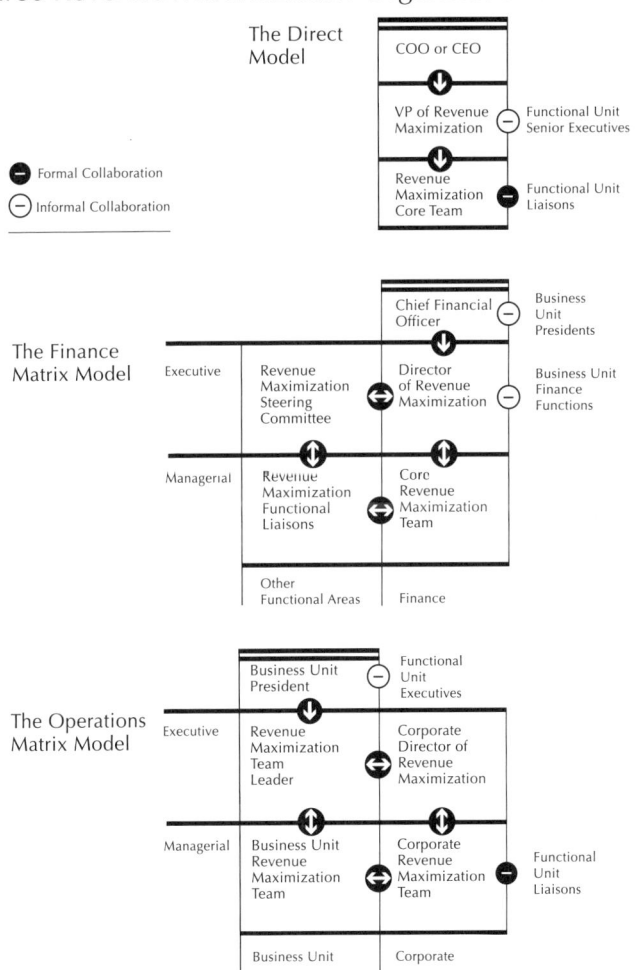

The main disadvantage of this structure is that it tends to work only for smaller companies with less diffuse organizational structures.

THE FINANCE MATRIX MODEL

Larger companies, with far-flung business units and huge functional organizations, frequently turn to organizational matrices to promote specific ends. The same is true of revenue maximization. In the first matrix model (the finance matrix model) the finance function *drives* revenue maximization. To achieve the collaborative participation of the entire organization, the matrix links these finance-area drivers to an executive-level revenue maximization steering committee and to managerial functional experts.

Because the function reports to the CFO, the company achieves P&L ownership of revenue maximization through the CFO's direct responsibility for overall corporate profitability. CFOs tend to be motivated because revenue maximization gives them a way to contribute measurably to corporate profitability, integrity, and growth. That, of course, is the idea. It only works if the CFO cares about maximizing revenue.

The primary goal of the finance matrix, however, is collaborative participation, not P&L ownership. According to its proponents, the model's main benefit is the "neutrality" it engenders for revenue maximization. Qwest, for instance, houses its revenue maximization function in finance. Pat Walker explained to us that other functions thus "see us as neutral. They see that we just want to get problems resolved. They are also comfortable that we don't have an axe to grind. If we were in an individual function, it would have been viewed with more suspicion."

THE OPERATIONS MATRIX MODEL

The operations matrix does not entail replacing the word finance in the above with the word operations. In the operations matrix model, the management of individual business units drives revenue maximization. Each unit may house smaller revenue maximization teams, but the *corporate* revenue maximization function exists to accelerate individual business units' efforts with expertise and additional resources.

Telecom companies including Bell Canada and Verizon have adopted the operations matrix. Advocates of this model believe that only P&L owners, with the deep incentive of finding the incremental revenue necessary to meet their own growth targets, can move their organization to greater revenue maximization commitment. They also strongly argue that the operations areas have the process improvement experience necessary for preventive capture. Finally, they point out that the P&L owners have the clout to get participation of functional units through informal channels. (The corporate revenue maximization function, however, often brings in functional collaboration through formal links between functional experts and the core team.)

These corporate revenue maximization functions serve as a vital corporate resource. At Verizon, explained Karin Wagar of her corporate function (housed in IT), "We are like consultants to the business lines. We try to be the first source of tool development for them. We also have experience to see early warnings of problems, such as through billing errors. We bring that evidence to them."

An admission: all the models are a little too clean. For revenue maximization as for many new corporate initiatives, the organizational structure tends to evolve from actions, not from playing with an org chart. For example, some operations matrix companies have a corporate revenue maximization function, but business unit functions in only a handful of divisions. Why? Because some divisions don't want a function. Other companies have their own particular hybrid. AT&T, for example, has established a sort of operations matrix, which is light on the matrix. The leading revenue maximizing divisions have established core teams around particular initiatives. The corporate "revenue assurance management" team consults with the business units but concentrates most of its energy on credits and collections, accounts receivable issues, and billing operations.

Two questions

Two questions about the models remain. First, which model do we prefer? Second, where, if not in finance, should a company place its corporate revenue maximization function?

Our vote... We used to be strong finance matrix partisans, as we had seen great success when the CFO's organization drove revenue maximization (either in smaller companies or in relatively autonomous business units). Steering committees at early revenue maximizers also proved invaluable in ensuring collaborative participation. Yet the passion and conviction of companies like Bell Canada and their operations-driven model are hard to ignore.

So we won't. With a politician's smooth cop-out, we vote for the model that best suits a company's needs. Obviously, a company with acute revenue leakage (and a tighter organizational structure) may need the direct model's cabinet-level senior revenue maximization executive. A company whose greatest challenge is ensuring collaboration may need the neutrality of the finance-model matrix. And a company most concerned about making revenue maximization a top priority may need the business unit leadership of the operations matrix model.

If not finance, then where? The location of an independent corporate revenue maximization function is less important than its features. Some companies, with existing Six Sigma or process improvement functions, have natural homes for the initiative. Other companies have had success placing revenue maximization in the IT function. This structure allows them, they argue, better access to technical expertise. (One executive whose company houses the initiative in IT further argued to us, "In some organizations, finance is thought of as a bean counter. And operations may be too close to the problem.")

Obviously, we prefer that a company place a corporate revenue maximization function in the area, like process improvement, that can best ensure participation of other functions without crashing into the defensiveness, pride, and skepticism of the silo mentality. There are two other important guidelines for best locating the function. First, the function's home and leadership should be, all else being equal, as high in the organization as possible. (If a revenue maximization czar is three or four levels below the head of billing, IT, or marketing, the function's organizational location will be the least of its problems.) Second, in the early stages of revenue maximization at least, function should follow enthusiasm. The organization shouldn't simply assign a grumbling executive to a task he or she doesn't much care for. ("I have to do *what?*") It's better to allow an early champion—a wild-eyed zealot rising out of a successful project in the dabbler phase—to form the nucleus of a core team.

How about internal audit? One historically common home for revenue maximization-like activities in the telecom, cable, and utilities industries has been internal audit. A few arguments for this structure exist. First, many skills overlap between internal auditors and revenue maximizers (such as the forensic bent), and internal auditors generally, on a gut level, understand the importance of the tactics to make revenue collection timely, accurate, and complete. Second, some internal audit functions, such as BellSouth's, have proven that internal audit can achieve success with revenue maximization projects.

However, the arguments against placing revenue maximization in internal audit are probably stronger. Above all, it *hasn't* worked at most companies. As one telecom executive told us, "Our revenue assurance function started with borrowed members from our audit group. And the people in the company treated it like an audit. You couldn't get any traction from the operations group—they would put up barriers." Right or wrong, internal auditors, who are responsible for operational and financial controls, are often viewed as "cops" by other functions, and others in the company are unlikely to view any initiative associated with internal audit as a strategy for increased profitability and growth. It would be a strange day when a product manager sought someone from internal audit to help her minimize leakage during a product launch.

Actions a company can take now

Before we recommend specific actions, we want to discuss briefly the different experiences small and large companies have had maximizing revenue. Smaller companies have been more successful in becoming revenue responsible organizations. They simply have less organizational inertia, fewer organizational overlaps, and more concentrated organizational leadership. They can move quicker and in tighter lockstep. Some hospitals, for example, have been able to maximize revenue relatively rapidly. While they still face conflicts between the patient financial services and patient care sides of the house, they don't have to face individual functional units of 8,000 employees spread throughout a country, as large telecom companies do. In the telecom and cable industries, too, smaller organizations with committed leadership have tended to move quicker toward the revenue responsible organization. Oftentimes, smaller companies have achieved more because they have less. A resource-poor initiative, which can't invest in long-term "giant leap" solutions, will avoid the snares of imagining a company can conquer revenue leakage with expensive systems upgrades. Poorer initiatives will often be "savvier" and achieve considerable success with homegrown tools and quick-win process improvement projects.

We recommend below actions that all companies, small or large, can take to become revenue responsible organizations.

1. **Define revenue maximization.** Defining revenue maximization clearly as an initiative that can bolster profitability, integrity, and growth can start a company on

the road to becoming a revenue responsible organization. As Pat Walker of Qwest told us, "Just the definition alone can help you sell it."

2. **Make one person in the organization accountable.** A company doesn't need a formal function from the beginning, but early on, it probably needs at least one person with some clout who will be responsible for revenue maximization. When we asked Terry Mosey of Bell Canada what he would advise a beginner company to do, he answered, "I would suggest to them that you get an individual that is director-level or preferably a VP. Tell that person that your job is revenue assurance. That's the only reason to get up, that's the only reason you're going to get paid, and that's the only reason you're going to be employed by this company. Send out an organizational announcement that this person is going to be an ongoing agenda item at management meetings. He has to talk for 15 minutes at each and every meeting. If the individual doesn't have 15 minutes of things to say, then there will be a lot of minutes of silence at each and every meeting."

3. **Beg for or borrow resources for a diagnostic or pilot project.** Early champions must be relentless in obtaining seed money for the first revenue maximization projects.

4. **Pick a pilot project that crosses at least one boundary.** If a pilot project only involves the billing function, for instance, a company will not be able to use the project's success to foster collaborative participation.

5. **Systematically identify targets for informal persuasion.** A company doesn't need an executive level steering committee from the first day, but early revenue maximization champions should take pains to identify people who will eventually need to come aboard the train.
6. **Worry about structure at the right time.** A beginner company should not spend its early energy worrying about an elegant organizational structure. It should spend its early energy pursuing quick wins, capturing revenue, generating enthusiasm, and managing success. A more advanced company should worry about the structure, though. It should assess its revenue maximization resource needs and its corporate culture. It should methodically develop, from the bottom up, a specific "best possible" structural plan to create a revenue responsible organization.
7. **Charter a formal, best-practice revenue assurance function.** A company should thoughtfully choose the makeup and home for the function.
8. **Integrate revenue maximization into budgeting and compensation processes.** Revenue maximization projects need people and money. In the long term, the necessary resources should be allocated up front in the normal budgeting process. (The same is true for the revenue and profit gains from the initiative.) Similarly, if individuals in an organization are to be held accountable, a company must formally write revenue maximization into its compensation and personal target structures.

9. **Change the culture.** Obviously, "changing the culture" is not a legal act, like changing your spouse. It's more like changing your children. There are countless experts on training, internal marketing, and other mechanisms of changing. We would only add to these specific tactics our general success factors. And we reiterate the importance, infusing this entire book, of leadership. As Steve Kloeblen of IBM said to us about the great focus on revenue leakage he has helped lead, "Cultural change has been through the leadership team and through repeated communication. We have to have a consistent message—a consistent drumbeat—and *show* the change."

Notes

1. Welch, *Jack: Straight from the Gut*, 56.
2. Pande, Neuman, and Cavanagh, *The Six Sigma Way*, 113.
3. Welch, *Jack: Straight from the Gut*, 332.

CHAPTER TEN

QUANTIFIABLE MONITORING MECHANISMS

What gets measured gets done, has long been the informal motto of our practice. (We recently learned that this had been first said long ago by the oddly-named organizational theorist Mason Hare.[1]) We should probably amend the motto to "gets done right," for as metrics-enthusiast Pat Walker of Qwest said to us, "Until you have something monitored and accepted, you keep on *redoing* it over and over again. Metrics give you the necessary accountabilities."

Quantifiable monitoring mechanisms are a core strategic focus of revenue maximization. But, unlike a detective tool project, a process gap project, or a cultural change project, a metrics project will rarely produce benefits except as it leads to the more precise and urgent application of one of the other core strategies. (That's why we put it, graphically, outside the circle.) **As Figure 10.1 illustrates, monitoring mechanisms bond and embed the other core strategies by managing—enabling—a living cycle of measured process improvement, tool implementation, and organizational commitment.**

Figure 10-1
Quantifiable Monitoring Mechanisms Bond and Embed All Strategies

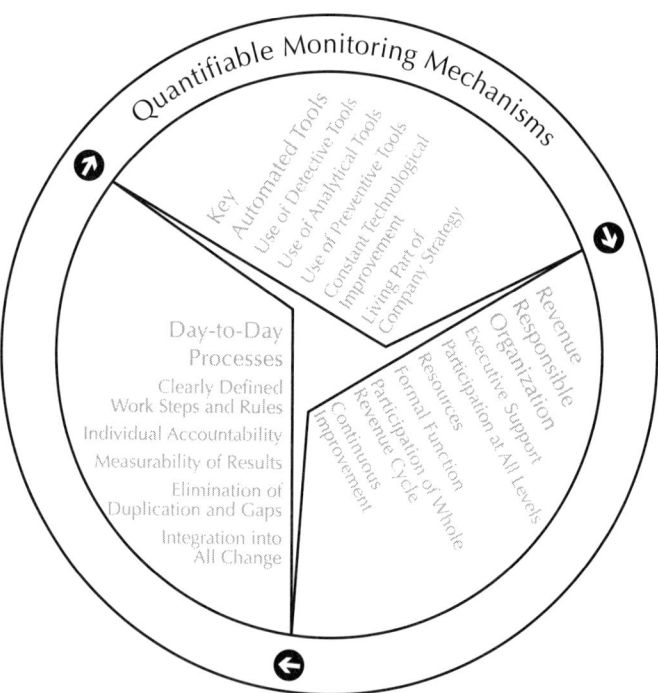

As in the formal organizational structures discussed in the last chapter, establishing quantifiable monitoring mechanisms should not be a day one activity. One telecom company, for instance, put together a new core revenue maximization team whose very first project was, inadvisably, the construction of a major new metrics system. The company had put the cart before the horse. Revenue maximization metrics will not lead to any captured revenue at a still-resistant company, and the core team had no authority and no buy-in from the organization.

That being said, a revenue maximization initiative must embrace embryonic forms of a monitoring program from the beginning. Most importantly, it must foster a culture of measurement so that individual revenue maximization projects and processes are habitually, in the natural course of events, quantified.

Water, water everywhere, and not a drop to drink. Most companies, floating on an ocean of metrics, are still thirsty for ones that truly improve operations. Telecom companies, for instance, have buckets of metrics—metrics for call centers, metrics for network operations, and metrics for financial performance. Some companies probably have metrics for average toes per employee and coat hangers per closet. Yet few companies use metrics to ensure that they collect all the revenue and only the revenue they deserve, and few apply revenue leakage-related metrics in a best-practice way to their operations, processes, and systems. Big-picture revenue maximization metrics like those listed in Table 10.1 are not only vital for discrete revenue maximization initiatives, they can also help a company better understand the confluence of financial and operational performance. They can help push a company to excellence, that is if a company develops a thoughtful metrics program like our "Simplify, Integrate, and Tier" approach and if a company follows some basic guiding principles.

Table 10.1
Sample Tier 1 Revenue Maximization Metrics

Telecom
- Dropped calls compared to total calls and average call duration
- Number of calls entering mediation versus number purged
- Dollar value of invoice errors as percentage of total invoice value
- Total value of customer credits

Electric Utilities
- Number of incoming calls and disputes
- Number of cancel/rebills performed monthly
- Billed usage as percentage of expected usage
- Percentage of billing errors caused by third-party data

Healthcare
- Total value of point-of-service cash collection
- Total amount of payer denials
- Open accounts per collector
- Total accounts receivable greater than 90 days

Why monitoring mechanisms are important

Revenue maximization monitoring mechanisms exist, above all else, to provide management with meaningful, quantified, and repeated snapshots of enterprisewide revenue leakage and revenue maximization performance. Through these snapshots, the monitoring mechanisms impel a company to perform the actions necessary to maximize revenue further. Metrics only work, and should only exist, if they lead to preventive or immediate revenue capture.

Metrics do lead to captured revenue. At one hospital our colleagues worked with, the organization's financial health was in jeopardy from acute revenue leakage. This was no backwater hospital; from a medical innovation standpoint, it was one of the finest in the United States. Yet its financial problems became so dire that its board of directors threatened to remove top management, and top management, attached to the concept of being employed, sought outside assistance. With that help, the hospital diagnosed itself, redesigned major processes, acquired automated tools, established new revenue maximization processes, and, crucially, integrated a dashboard with 12 high-level revenue cycle-related key performance indicators (KPIs) into its operations. Management began to report these KPIs monthly to the board of directors. The metrics helped bond and accelerate the initiatives, which together brought the hospital's receivables down by 40 days and increased its cash flow by 20 percent.

Monitoring mechanisms help—in some cases, enable—a company to maximize revenue in five specific ways. Monitoring mechanisms:

1. Concentrate management focus on revenue maximization
2. Provide quick analysis and alerts of "hot button" issues
3. Improve progress and planning of specific strategies
4. Align employees to corporate revenue maximization goals with formal accountability tied to metrics
5. Link together disparate strategies with enterprisewide and operational measures of success

SIMPLIFY, INTEGRATE, TIER

How should a company get a drop to drink from the ocean of metrics? We recommend a three-pronged approach:

- **Simplify** the inputs and outputs of monitoring mechanisms.
- **Integrate** metrics into the operations and organization.
- **Tier** metrics by management level.

All three prongs of the simultaneous approach convert loose metrics jingling around a company's pockets into a monitoring mechanism essential to maximizing revenue.

SIMPLIFY

"Simplicity, simplicity, simplicity!" railed Thoreau from Walden Pond. And so, too, do we when it comes to designing revenue maximization monitoring mechanisms. Companies should simplify how they acquire metrics and how each individual views them.

Simplify the acquisition of metrics. The basic data for monitoring mechanisms can come from three sources: existing automated metrics, tool-generated metrics, and manually calculated metrics. Companies should develop monitoring programs only around metrics in these categories that can be simply and repeatedly acquired.

For metrics that are already (and often automatically) gathered, companies should simplify the day-to-day process to ensure that metrics straightforwardly and consistently reach the individual or team responsible for monitoring mechanisms. Companies should also ensure that the monitoring processes are in sync with existing processes to gather metrics from operational data. If, for instance, a utility's engineering function collects data on the first of every month, the managers of a monitoring program should use that data when it's available and not ask for it on the tenth.

Additional metrics generated by new detective tools can be invaluable for a monitoring program. Companies should feed data produced by these tools into larger monitoring mechanisms only *after* they make a particular tool a living part of their operations. Companies needing to produce a quarterly metrics report by the next day will probably have a tough time finding a person able to wave a magic wand, bend time, and rerun, overnight, a two-month detective tool project.

Certain metrics are hand-calculated. For example, in the telecom industry, we have worked with companies to measure "product development effectiveness," a metric to determine if new products are effectively and correctly launched by measuring sub-metrics like the number of product launches meeting established time parameters and the amount of incremental customer-care activity surrounding product launches. While these metric and sub-metrics can be extremely useful in an enterprisewide corporate monitoring program, they don't fall out of a system after tickling a couple of keystrokes. Thus, if a company chooses to calculate new, more difficult metrics, as an aggressive company will, it must surround this calculation with documented, practical processes.

Simplify viewing metrics. Simplicity is as important to the outputs of a monitoring program as it is to the inputs. In Chapter 8, we strongly recommended implementing a dashboard analytical tool. Dashboards have proven their value at a few leading healthcare companies and selected areas of telecom companies. Web-based technology makes the dashboards easy to update and widely distribute.

During the development of almost every metrics-design program, some zealot insists that this or that person must vigilantly monitor 25 metrics or it will die a long, horrible death from metrics deprivation. In our experience, to the contrary, when an organization formally expects an individual executive or manager to pay active attention to more than 10 or 12 metrics, the individual ends up paying attention to none.

INTEGRATE

A best-practice monitoring mechanism strategy will integrate metrics into operations and into a company's organization.

Integrate into operations. Pat Walker argued forcefully to us that, "If metrics don't link back to operational measures, they fail." Even more so, "If metrics don't point to process issues then they are fairly useless." Pat recommends implementing high-level KPIs, but she more passionately advocates operational metrics that can point to specific sources of leakage and specific operational fixes. A mid-level metric that calculates how many exceptions are being purged from a billing system, for instance, will immediately compel action if the exceptions jump from 2,000 in one month to 20,000 in the next.

Managers of monitoring mechanisms must remain vigilant in looking for aberrant results from individual measurements. More importantly, they must follow up to ensure that the *metrics move in the right direction.* That is, monitoring alerts must lead to preventive capture through immediate action, day-to-day process improvement, or preventive tools. All the innovation behind New York's rigorous Compstat crime measurement initiative would have accomplished little if a precinct captain, alerted to the exploding number of bicycle thefts in his precinct, complimented the Compstat managers on the niftiness of their computers but didn't put out an APB on the Bicycle Bandit.

Integrate into the organization. Metrics must also be hooked into the organization. A best-practice enterprisewide monitoring program will calculate metrics for managing initiatives *and* formally integrate them into the operational targets of individual managers. The manager of a customer care function should be held accountable if exceptions "spit out" from a billing system jumped to 20,000 from 2,000 in one month because, for instance, his customer care team decided, as a group joke, to insert "3" as every customer's last name.

Hooking metrics into the organization also requires informal hooks. Companies must make sure that people understand, trust, and internalize the numbers. This takes education and training, and it takes good design of the monitoring mechanisms themselves.

Some companies that didn't integrate metrics into the organization faced considerable resistance. At a few telecom companies, for example, a monitoring program was too large for the organization. Monitoring was thus seen as a somewhat sinister, outsider, watchdog function rather than as a regular program by which managers and executives could view the business and improve profitability, integrity, and growth. One telecom company spent millions of dollars trying to create new metrics, but, because the metrics weren't seen as tools to improve operations, they gathered virtual dust in yet another data warehouse.

Tier

How do you simplify *and* integrate? Tiering executive, managerial, and supervisory metrics throughout an organization can create a monitoring mechanism that both simplifies each individual's relations to a metrics program and integrates metrics into the operations and organization. However, a robust tiered monitoring mechanism doesn't come out of a box like a new toy train. Constructing one demands a sophisticated, cross-functional effort. But once it is created, a tiered monitoring strategy can truly bond and embed every part of an organization's pursuit of revenue maximization.

We call executive-level metrics "Tier 1," manager-level metrics "Tier 2," and supervisor-level metrics "Tier 3." The road from Tier 3 to Tier 1 is not uniform and involves three types of tiering:

- **Tiering by aggregation.** Tiering at its simplest aggregates metrics from lower-level divisions, geographic areas, or work units. Thus an airline's attempt to calculate wrongly-exchanged seats would aggregate total company performance in a Tier 1 metric, a particular region in a Tier 2 metric, and an airport shift in a Tier 3 metric.

- **Tiering by calculation.** More complicated tiering involves calculating new metrics from two or more sub-metrics. In the example illustrated in Figure 10.2, the percentage of a company's total commission sales not provisioned is an important Tier 1 metric, for instance, for executives at technology services companies and in the business customer divisions of telecom companies. Many companies don't calculate this metric now but can derive it from Tier 2 metrics like total commission sales validated by internal processes and total revenue of services activated. (In some cases, such as "product launch effectiveness" discussed above, the calculations are significantly more complicated than simple addition. Doing them demands technical expertise.)

- **Tiering by amplification.** Many Tier 2 and Tier 3 metrics, however, have no mathematical relation to higher metrics. They merely (but importantly) amplify those higher metrics. Thus a senior manager, who is accountable for the Tier 2 metric (as illustrated in Figure 10.2) of the number of services orders deployed, will be concerned if that number deviates one month from the trend. Consulting a Tier 3 metric like backlog of service orders may alert her to underlying operational problems.

We have seen some companies make strides in tiering metrics, but we are not aware of any company, at least in the telecom and related industries, that has sewn together a sophisticated tiered monitoring mechanism. Why? Tiering mechanisms are difficult and often demand skilled, full-time employees to manage them on a daily basis. But once completed, the tiering strategy will allow a company to simplify metrics and hold each individual accountable for 10 or 12 performance indicators. It will also, we hope, allow companies to integrate metrics and create energetic procedures to convert metrics into action. A best-practice tiered monitoring mechanism, which is the stuff of our occasional daydreams, would add point-and-click "investigative" functions to a graphical, Web-based, widely-distributed dashboard. With such capability, an executive concerned about a Tier 1 metric could click onto lower tier metrics to get a better view of the situation.

Figure 10.2
Sample Tiered Metrics

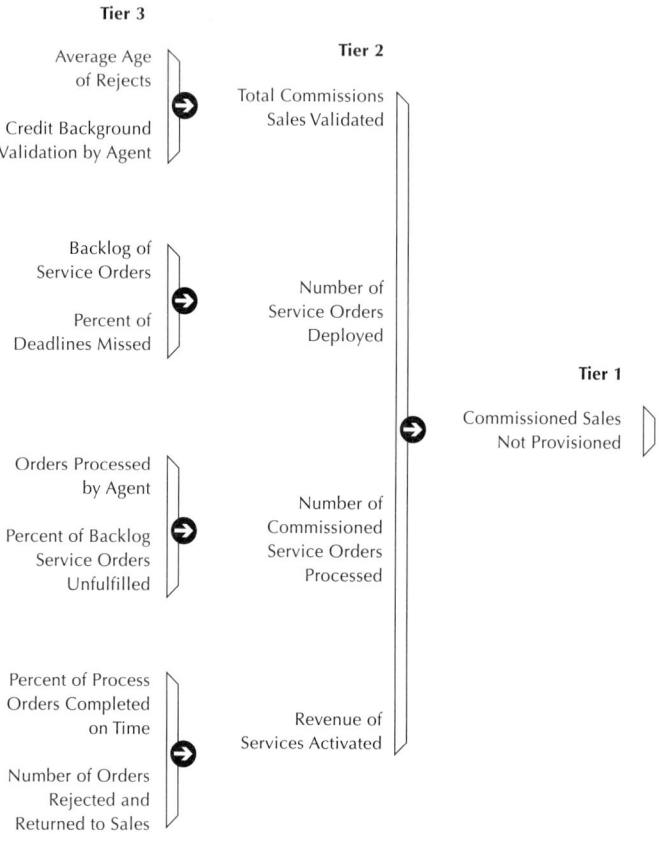

An elusive fourth tier? We also daydream about another metric, the Measured Effective Revenue Integrity Rate (MERIR)—an enterprisewide measure of *total* revenue maximized. A company with an MERIR of 99.5 percent, for instance, would leak 0.5 percent of total revenue. In the telecom industry, the MERIR is as elusive as Bigfoot and, perhaps also like Bigfoot, lives only in the imagination. For the past three years, we have written and occasionally talked about the concept, and we have received little response other than congratulations on our ability to think of moderately clever acronyms. We strongly suspect, however, that as leading companies establish best-practice tiered monitoring mechanisms, they will acquire enough data on a regular basis and enough metric-manipulation skills to be able finally, with a big smile, to look in the MERIR.

Guiding principles for quantifiable monitoring mechanisms

Establishing monitoring mechanisms under the simplify, integrate, tier approach is not an easy task. Like changing a company's organizational structure, it should be attempted only after riding a wave of momentum and success. A company should periodically calculate and update metrics, be realistic and concentrate on the trend, and fight for monitoring mechanisms.

Periodically calculate and update metrics

One-time calculations of data can be valuable, of course. First runs of detective tools, for example, frequently find millions of dollars in immediate revenue capture opportunities. Yet quantifiable monitoring mechanisms that manage a revenue maximization initiative are not merely diagnostic tools. A company must calculate key metrics, depending on their complexity, on a weekly, monthly, or quarterly basis.

Equally important, a revenue responsible organization must regularly adjust its metrics for accuracy. Companies with robust metrics for other initiatives—for instance, cost reduction or customer satisfaction—have established continuous metric evaluation processes. Revenue maximizing companies should follow a similar, documented approach, which:

- Produces metrics reports
- Analyzes report values to highlight areas of operational concern
- Evaluates metrics standards to determine if metrics are operationally useful
- Updates report standards before reports are produced again

Be Realistic: concentrate on the trend

"Do something" is a particularly relevant success factor for revenue maximization monitoring strategies. Many companies we have observed fall into the trap of perfection when designing metrics. They spend so much time tuning their instruments that they never play a note. Companies that have experienced the most success with metrics worry more about integrating the metrics into operations and less about mathematical precision. Revenue maximization monitoring mechanisms are not measurements for audit purposes. They are tools to capture the opportunities within a company.

Many metrics can be calculated three or four different ways, and, frequently, fiercely, personal debates erupt over the choice of calculations. Few things frustrate us more than a company taking six or nine months to agree upon a metric. Some companies also delay implementing metrics because of worries about data quality. If a detective tool, for instance, produces a small number of incorrect records on a periodic basis, companies fret over whether those records are *really* incorrect and what the definition of "incorrect" is.

It doesn't matter. Companies must concentrate on the *trend* of an individual metric, not its absolute value. As long as the detective tool is run the same way every month, it will produce a report based on the same, however imperfect, rules every month. A company shouldn't get itself into a knot over whether a billing accuracy percentage is, for example, 98.1 percent or, in a different method of calculation, 98.5 percent. It should watch like a hawk, though, to make sure a billing accuracy percentage isn't 98.1 percent in December, 98.2 percent in January, 98.0 percent in February, and 91.0 percent in March.

Furthermore, the more intricate a metric is, the less transparent it will probably be, and the more organizational resistance it will get from people who doubt the value of a revenue maximization monitoring program. Individual metrics must not be esoteric new calculations. People have to believe in the numbers, and they have to understand them.

Fight for quantifiable monitoring mechanisms

If all four core strategies were sitting on the sidelines before a pickup game of basketball, people would always pick metrics last. As we said, people just don't like them. In the telecom industry, for instance, less progress has been made on metrics than on any of the other core strategies.

The resistance comes from two fronts. First, executives complain that they already have too many metrics—metrics spilling out of their eyes and ears and noses—no matter how useless or academic some of these existing metrics may be.

Second, executives, and especially managers, are leery of new metrics because they recognize, accurately, that metrics exist in the long run to hold people accountable. At many telecom companies, for instance, some functions delay supplying (or even refuse altogether to give) the needed data to a revenue maximization team because they are suspicious of the team's motives for wanting the data.

We have seen lots of fights about metrics in the telecom and related industries. Many of the squabbles come from different silos championing different ways to calculate metrics, each silo fighting for the calculation method that shows itself in the best light. At one telecom company, it took 18 months for the various functions to agree on a metrics program. Another European telecom company experienced battles over what to call certain metrics. The billing department fiercely resisted the term "billing accuracy" and was finally pacified with "event capture." Fighting for metrics requires the same leadership and relentlessness, as any revenue maximization program, if not more. One telecom executive finally got so fed up by a maddening, mulish debate about calculating metrics that she drew a line in the sand and dictated how metrics would be calculated. However, ingeniously, she told the various functions that they would not be held accountable to the new metrics *for one year*, giving them time to adjust to the concept and understand the trends.

Actions a company takes now

1. **Promote a culture of measurement from day one.** In the preceding chapters, we talked about measurability: measurability of results in day-to-day processes, measured participation of all layers of management, measured leakage from detective tools. The vigorous,

intelligent pursuit of the other core strategies should produce a culture of measurement. As individual projects generate metrics that are eventually tied into larger monitoring mechanisms, the habit of constant measurement readies an organization to implement more sophisticated revenue maximization metrics. A best-practice monitoring program will be welcomed as a tool to grow revenue and profits, rather than feared as an instrument of torture.

2. **Capture at least one new metric with every implemented tool.** For example, if a cable company regularly runs a provision check tool, it should capture the periodic output of that effort, such as the number of cable boxes turned on but not billed.

3. **Design two *new* metrics, calculate them, and socialize them within the company.** Metrics champions must, early on, actively work the organization to gain support for monitoring mechanisms. It's better to begin this project with two metrics than with a brick-sized report containing dozens.

4. **Build a tiering strategy.** This is a major project, as we said, and often requires outside help. It is necessary, however, for advanced companies.

5. **Integrate quantifiable monitoring mechanisms into the compensation structure.** It won't be initially popular, but it must be done over the long term.

6. **Take certain KPIs to the board, shareholders, and analyst community.** Above, we said that KPIs are tools to help a company maximize revenue, not audited figures. Nevertheless, if a company integrates certain KPIs into its operations and organization and judges itself on the trends of those KPIs, it should, like the

once-struggling hospital, commit itself to improving the KPIs to board of directors and, in some cases, to shareholders and the investment community.

7. **Build a graphical, Web-based dashboard.** A few outside vendors and strategic advisors combine expertise in the technical design of dashboards and, more importantly, the design of metrics programs feeding them.

8. **"Measure things to death."** Bell Canada's Pete Varley, when sharing his general thoughts on revenue maximization, advised companies to "measure things to death." This advice is literally true. The purpose of metrics, of quantifiable monitoring mechanisms, is to measure leakage and operational problems *to death*— to create such a robust, continuous, looping program of measurement and operational improvement that revenue leakage and revenue collection inaccuracies wither to as close to zero as possible.

NOTES

1. Peters and Waterman, *In Search of Excellence*, 268.

CHAPTER ELEVEN

IDENTIFY, QUANTIFY, CAPTURE

The four core strategies we discussed in the last four chapters—integrating revenue maximization into day-to-day processes, implementing key automated tools, creating a revenue responsible organization, and bonding all these with quantifiable monitoring mechanisms—are what all companies must do, to some extent, at *every* phase of revenue maximization to capture the opportunity to improve profitability, integrity, and growth. They are what enthusiastic companies have done forcefully. They are also the ingredients of almost every individual revenue maximization project.

This chapter elaborates on a concept we introduced earlier: the recipe steps of identify, quantify, capture, as detailed in Figure 11.1. We and our colleagues have applied this approach to help turn the ingredients of the four core strategies into captured revenue. Many project approaches offer similar steps, but ours, proven in battle, offers a few key advantages. It is simple and easily understood by the organization. It's applicable on both a macro (enterprisewide initiative) and micro (individual project) basis. Unlike some other projects that seem to consist of a three-step "grumble, bumble, and stumble" approach from lack of conviction, lack of direction, and lack of purpose, this approach focuses a project on the all-important end goal of revenue capture. Finally, and perhaps most important, the identify, quantify, capture approach encourages a company to maximize revenue in stages, addressing the best opportunities first, and actively managing the risk of its investment. (The approach, by the way, also applies to most corporate initiatives pursuing quantifiable financial goals.)

Figure 11.1
Identify, Quantify, Capture Approach

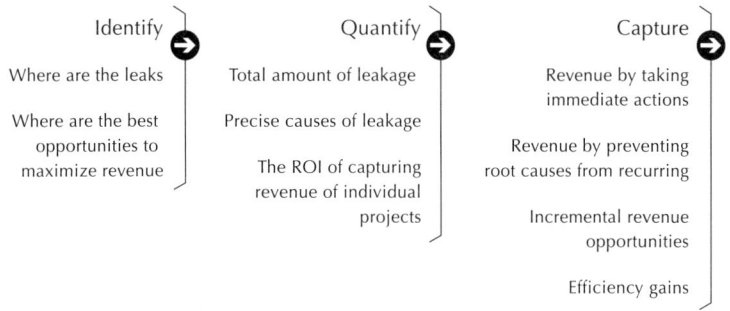

Step #1: identify

While identifying revenue leakage and revenue maximization opportunities is a more explicit step in a macro initiative than in a single project, a separate step to identify problems and opportunities does occur at the start of individual projects. In many cases, the identification of opportunities "bubbles up," in Karin Wagar's words, in a revenue responsible organization constantly seeking to maximize revenue. Similarly, monitoring mechanisms exist precisely to identify operational sources of leakage. Whatever the trigger, a project identification phase goes beyond simply choosing a project. Quantifying revenue leakage demands investment, and so a project's identification step must come before quantification and build the business case with some level of formality and intellectual rigor.

Formal diagnostics

Most companies with which we've been involved begin their growth-oriented revenue maximization experience with a formal diagnostic. (Of course, almost all companies, even in the resistant or dabbler phases, have done some revenue maximization activities before they attempt to address leakage enterprisewide.) The value of a diagnostic lies in its ability to unearth and, importantly, prioritize a broad array of revenue maximization opportunities. As Barbara Gibson of Interland told us, "Initially, the biggest barrier our revenue assurance program had was that there was so much to do. We really found the value in the diagnosis to be prioritizing our needs and seeing what we could address to achieve quick hits and what we could do longer term." A formal diagnostic can take many forms, but best-practice diagnostics contain some common features. They all:

- **Incorporate the wisdom of people in the field.** Managers and frontline employees often know about the ongoing glitches in company processes, have insights into the sources of revenue leakage, and can propose general solutions. (A few feel liberated when their companies finally begin addressing the low hanging fruit that they have, due to inertia, long tolerated.) To gather this information, those who conduct the diagnostic must be extraordinarily careful to position revenue maximization correctly—as the first step in a revenue growth initiative, not as an audit, not as a "consulting" project to see how costs (and people) can be removed, not as one function trying to figure out what's going wrong in other functions, and especially not as an investigation into why certain individuals have allowed leakage. A diagnostic should not, for example, be conducted by interrogators in dark glasses, in a windowless basement room with a single, naked bulb shining in an employee's face. (A sample diagnostic question appears in Table 11.1.)
- **Diagnose a company holistically to understand misalignments, disagreements, misconceptions, and gaps.** A good doctor does more than read your blood pressure and put it silently into a chart, and a good diagnostic systematically compares answers from different functions to locate flaws or gaps in corporate processes. This comparison often results in the quick wins we talked about in Chapter 7.

Table 11.1
Sample Telecom Industry Diagnostic Question

Are exceptions and errors in the activation process corrected on a timely basis?

HIGHLIGHTS

- [ ] Sales agents are notified electronically of rejected service orders
- [ ] Personnel are responsible for monitoring the status of rejections and rejection queues
- [ ] Aged rejection reports are reviewed and followed up on a regular basis
- [ ] Key data fields are controlled using format and expected results

OPPORTUNITIES

- [ ] No reporting performed on rejected service orders
- [ ] Sales agents do not have order entry capability
- [ ] Hardcopy versions of service order documentation are manually transferred between sales and order management group
- [ ] No segregation between sales and approval groups/personnel

- **Benchmark.** Diagnostics can't be solipsistic exercises. They must compare a company to others in its industry (and sometimes other industries), usually by methodically ranking a company against industry averages and the best in class.

- **Are practical-minded.** We have often seen diagnostics that are high-level fluff. Although a diagnostic, by definition, doesn't go into the transactional details of inaccurate, untimely, or incomplete collection of revenue, those conducting it must be exceedingly aware of its practical implications by prioritizing immediately actionable projects, by doing back-of-the-envelope calculations on discovered opportunities, and by revealing quick-win projects. A diagnostic that doesn't reveal at least a few quick-win projects should probably be immediately filed in the trash.

- **Are quickly done.** In our experience in the telecom industry, a robust diagnostic can be performed in three to five weeks of intense, focused analysis.
- **Are viewed as a checkup, not an operation.** Many beginner companies start their path to commitment with a formal diagnostic. Enthusiast companies have robust, quantifiable monitoring mechanisms that, in essence, continually diagnose the company. Yet it could easily take a beginner company four or five years to reach the enthusiast phase, and we recommend that companies diagnose themselves a few times in the interim. People, processes, and systems change so quickly that pursuing a revenue maximization plan on a three-year-old diagnostic could cause a company to march aggressively forward, with its flank exposed.

In Chapter 6, we touched upon the cases for internal versus external professionals conducting the diagnostic. Companies can and do perform internal diagnostics all the time (picking up, for example, peer comparisons at conferences), but most companies can benefit from an external, deeply experienced team that knows what questions to ask, can benchmark (from real data) a company against its peers, is perceived as neutral, and, like any good detective, can smell the leaks.

STEP #2: QUANTIFY

While the concept needs little explanation, quantification is a crucially important step because, in a sense, it *defines* revenue maximization as a high-return financial opportunity rather than as a vague efficiency strategy. A few years ago, many executives looked askance at an additional step dedicated to quantification. ("And how much is *that* gonna cost us?") Yet recently, in the industries we've worked with, companies have embraced quantification steps as essential. Back-of-the-envelope calculations are important, advisable, and a good use for old envelopes, but quantification exercises using detective and analytical tools are vital in isolating and tallying the details—not only *how much* a leak represents, but *what* the leak *is*. The move from back-of-the-envelope to robust quantification efforts is where many companies, looking for short cuts, trip up: they fail to put forth the demanded effort at this step to adequately prepare themselves for success and revenue capture. Energetically quantifying revenue leakage and revenue collection inaccuracies is the necessary step to put the enemy directly in the sniper's scope.

Project quantification. On a micro basis, projects must quantify revenue leakage, revenue capture opportunities, and needed investment to weigh those projects against other sources of revenue growth. The detective and analytical tools required in this step create new data, analyze existing data, and stratify data to:

- Assess the magnitude of leakage and errors
- Discover the details of individual leaks—the mispriced tickets by agent, the free cable services by customer, the dropped call records by network element
- Determine patterns and causes of leakage
- Estimate the ROI of capturing targeted revenue

Quantification projects are often launched in phases, with a sampling project prefacing a full-scale quantification of leakage. In other projects, the full-scale quantification is the bulk of the project's range and investment. For example, if an airline mines data from travel agents' ticketing records to quantify mis-pricing and fraud, the investment lies in the tapping and analysis of the data. The long-term capture solutions—improved systems, new communications and training programs, or the assistance of the local police force—are so broad and involve so much of the airline's business that they probably extend beyond the boundaries of revenue maximization.

Macro quantification. On a macro basis, a company should ideally quantify, at more or less the same time, the best opportunities arising from a diagnostic. Thoughtfully weighing the worthiness of one potential opportunity quantified with hard data against another opportunity, only diagnosed with best guesses is difficult. Quantifying enterprisewide opportunities also gives an organization a strong sense of the total benefit of revenue maximization. (For cost reasons, many companies do broad quantification through sampling rather than full detection.) One Australian company, for instance, after quantifying key areas with a series of detective tool pilot projects, decided that, conservatively, it could seize a $50 million opportunity in revenue maximization. This met the company's threshold for aggressive action, and it began to put in place the muscles—resources and organizational commitment—necessary for widespread success.

Step #3: capture

The capture step is obviously the most exciting one. It's where a company creates value. It's also, as should be clear by now, the hardest stage. Revenue leakage usually can't be cured with duct tape and good intentions. Long-term preventive capture often requires reengineering major processes or fostering organizational change. Even immediate capture often demands rigorous manual work. But immediate and preventive capture—along with opportunity and efficiency capture—maximize revenue and convert all the core strategies into real dollars and real value at the bottom line.

IMMEDIATE CAPTURE

Immediate capture is the golden boy of the capture family, for it brings home money directly and often in bulk. Immediate capture projects correct inaccurate transaction data by back billing for services already provided or billing correctly for recurring services.

The most immediate of immediate capture is back billing. Deciding whether or not to back bill is a difficult and fractious process. In our experience, many revenue maximization projects forgo back billing because of its obvious potential to chip away at customer satisfaction. (Even sending back bills tucked in flowery greeting cards and earnest messages about "Sorry about our mistake" probably won't mollify a lot of customers.) We have worked with project teams, however, that have tiptoed into back billing and found less resistance than expected. One unit of a telecom company, for instance, spent $4 million on a revenue maximization project that quantified nearly $15 million in revenue leaked because active customers weren't being billed at all or they weren't being billed for everything they ordered. The company decided to back bill $5 million of this leakage to thousands of customers and set up a process to deal with complaints. After the bills were sent out, the project team, like a coastal town, boarded-up the windows, and waited for the hurricane. Less than ten customers complained.

Companies can sometimes immediately capture revenue from recurring services with a proverbial flip of the switch, such as when a revenue maximization project corrects an inaccurate master rate table or charge description master. Sometimes, immediate capture can require flipping thousands of switches. For example, a provisioning project detecting customers who are not being correctly charged for services will usually require customer files to be altered one by one. (A few leading IT departments have become skilled at accelerating this immediate capture with on-the-fly, software programs that automate the fixes.)

Reducing accounts receivable offers another immediate opportunity for revenue capture. The revenue cycle, of course, begins at the point of sale and ends with cash coming in the door. For years, companies have launched credit and collections initiatives to reduce the aging of accounts receivable. (It's a rare company that says "forget about it" when a bill is not paid.) We have found that companies that perceive the reduction of receivables as revenue maximization—that is, as a proactive strategy—will more aggressively capture revenue, regardless of the fact that the economic benefits appear on the cash flow statement rather than the income statement. AT&T's revenue assurance management group, for example, spearheaded a major decline in accounts receivable using automated tools and a sophisticated program to ensure cooperation of its sales force. (In the healthcare industry, collections often take on a special urgency because Medicare, Medicaid, and other government payers will not pay a claim if it is still unresolved after two years, as many are.)

Finally, immediate capture can sometimes become tricky because of the complexity of the errors and fixes. For instance, a large telecom company we worked with suspected that its bills from local CLECs were inaccurate. In a pilot project, it looked at a single CLEC and discovered that the CLEC was overbilling the company by almost $1 million per year, well over 15 percent of the total charges. After looking at root causes and at the CLEC's billing systems, the company launched a tactical immediate capture project involving programming of systems on both sides of the transaction to better align call types and rate structures.

Preventive capture

Preventive capture projects prevent leaks from happening in the first place by addressing the proximate causes of leakage related to people, processes, and technology. Some projects also address cultural susceptibilities. (We've yet to find anyone who can address the temporal causes of leakage and make the world move more slowly.)

Process preventive capture. Day-to-day process improvement projects preventively capture revenue. For example, our colleagues worked with Johns Hopkins Medical Services Corporation to pioneer a best-practice "same-face-everywhere" process for patient registrars, unit secretaries, and admissions personnel. The goal was (is) to present the same face (message) in all patient access areas so when patients present to be treated, they receive a consistent customer service model. With heavy training in technology and procedures, with an aggressive competency screening program, with well-designed and easy-to-understand patient registration processes, with a robust monitoring mechanism linked to incentives and remedial training, the same-face- everywhere process significantly reduced errors and inaccuracies that had been directly responsible for delayed and denied payments. Other healthcare companies have since adopted the "franchise" process improvement tool.

In the airline industry, in which companies often think of preventive capture as "loss deterrence," almost all capture is preventive. All ticket purchases are discrete events, and most leakage is caused by human error, not systems glitches. (In a few cases, though, human error can have recurring consequences, such as the occasional mistyped fares found on some airline Web sites offering roundtrips from New York to Paris for $5.99, instead of $599.) The airline industry concentrates its preventive-capture focus on training and education (or the more ominous sounding, "behavior modification"), on process improvement, and on new preventive automated tools.

The paradox and the future of preventive tools. When we highlighted the growing power of preventive tools in Chapter 8, we cautioned against believing that major system improvements could be silver bullets that could stop all leakage. This caveat, in a sense, echoes Jim Collins' Stockdale Paradox—companies must operate on the assumption that all systems (including brand-new systems) cause leakage at the same time as they invest in long-term hope that the solution, the permanent preventive tool, will arrive. Of course, such a tool would never be able to eliminate human error, and it would need to be embedded into robust best-practice processes. Yet we can foresee a day, years from now, when a single tool will be developed. The powerful (and inevitably expensive) automated tool will be integrated into a company's operating backbone—for instance, the operational support system (OSS) in the telecom industry—and link together detective and analytical tools into a leak-preventing, monitoring, autocorrecting revenue capture system.

Organizational preventive capture. Preventive capture can also require cultural change. A cable company, for instance, can immediately capture revenue by making sure all customers receiving HBO are paying for it. But it takes harder preventive work to instill organizational commitment by holding provisioning managers accountable for provisioning-accuracy metrics or to summon the leadership necessary to spearhead a major reengineering of the provisioning processes.

Opportunity capture

In the introduction to this book, we said that we would mainly discuss direct leakage, not opportunity leakage because companies so far have primarily focused on and been rewarded by addressing direct leakage. But opportunity capture (and leakage) is gaining attention. Opportunity capture strategies help companies optimize their use of assets, enabling incremental sales to customers who are demanding services, with their wallets open. Leading companies are now, among other projects, optimizing networks to sell more services, systematically finding stranded assets and putting them to work, and eliminating basic inefficiencies in sales processes. For example, IBM's e-Business hosting unit launched a pilot process-improvement project to radically shorten customer provisioning time and first billing.

Opportunity capture often blends into other corporate initiatives like cost minimization or operating efficiency improvement. Electric utilities, for example, are now installing tools to better manage capacity to provide electricity during periods of peak demand. We have always thought of the failure to make these incremental peak sales as opportunity leakage. Many utilities, however, think of the failure mainly as an engineering problem.

Efficiency capture

Efficiency capture, in our terminology, is the most self-absorbed type of capture. It doesn't mean achieving operating efficiencies throughout the revenue cycle. Rather, it means capturing efficiencies *within the revenue maximization initiative itself.* Most executives we talked to shared experiences about reducing the headcount of billing departments or other areas performing heavy manual rework of transaction or service data. Much of this reduction comes about through automation, especially eliminating duplication—Terry Mosey's tongue-twisting "checkers checking checkers." The most satisfying capture comes from upstream improvements that negate manual work downstream.

There are obvious cost benefits to achieving these operating efficiencies, but the executives we spoke to stressed that the greatest benefit of efficiency capture was its ability to reallocate resources to profitability-oriented revenue maximizing activities.

THE CAVEATS: THE INEXACT SCIENCE OF ROI AND THE MELT FACTOR

The largest caveat for those employing the identify, quantify, capture approach is that although the stages are, metaphorically, recipe steps, following them isn't like baking a cake. It's more like making dinner for 500. We end this chapter with two other, more specific caveats. First, companies must be aware of the inexact nature of calculating the ROI of revenue maximization projects. Second, before launching a project, companies must understand the melt factor, in which captured revenue fails to meet the opportunity originally quantified.

THE INEXACT SCIENCE OF ROI

We've repeatedly stressed the importance of calculating the ROI of revenue maximization initiatives. The high ROI is one of the strategy's cardinal selling points—revenue maximization improves corporate profitability. However, calculating the ROI of individual projects isn't always an exact science. There are a few notable challenges:

- **Projects begin with imperfect data.** Many detective tool projects face considerable data challenges in verifying whether certain data indicates real errors and leaked transactions or merely a project's inability to completely reconcile different systems. A quantification project must proactively verify the amount of revenue leakage, but most projects stop short of achieving a penny-exact estimate. It's worthwhile to invest resources to quantify whether leakage is $18 million or $2 million. It's not worthwhile to invest them to determine if it's $18 million or $17 million. Oftentimes, then, a company begins capturing revenue before it knows exactly how much it's going to capture.

- **The return is often difficult to calculate.** Calculating the revenue captured in back billing is easy. Even calculating the net present value of the immediate capture of recurring charges can be straightforward. We have seen, though, team members argue about assumptions in these calculations, such as the estimate of how customer retention will be affected by the new, correct charges. (Many customers will no longer care so much for HBO when they no longer get it, accidentally, for free.) Isolating the precise returns of many revenue capture projects, especially preventive ones, is thorny. Establishing a "same face everywhere" patient registration improvement process will minimize delayed and denied payments. Yet other factors —a new major managed care contract, an acquisition, a change in personnel in a coding area—may muddy any attempt to establish direct causality and isolate the project's exact revenue impact.

- **The investment is often difficult to calculate.** The largest investment in most revenue maximization projects is people's time. Calculating the employee cost of a project team is simple. Calculating the employee cost can get murky, however, when large parts of an organization are involved. Some companies address this problem with intricate mechanisms to track the economic value of employee tasks, such as the activity-based costing method. However, most companies in these situations estimate rough employee cost or don't calculate ROI at all.

Sometimes, all these complicating factors work together to render pointless an effort to determine a project's ROI. AT&T's recent accounts receivable initiative, for example, produced astonishing economic benefits. Yet calculating the ROI was complicated by the trickiness of weighing cash flow against income statement benefits. More to the point, AT&T's revenue assurance management group succeeded by organizing the company's sales people to work actively on improving collections from enterprise accounts. Understandably, the company didn't worry about isolating the cost of the total sales force that should be considered an investment in the project.

The difficulties notwithstanding, companies do calculate the ROI as best they can. For example, some companies look primarily at the near-term "in-year" benefits of a revenue maximization project. (This calculation underplays the long-term benefits, but the in-year ROI is usually high enough to justify the project.) Other companies have attacked the challenges of calculating ROI with sophisticated project management techniques. In all this, companies should remember our advice concerning designing quantifiable monitoring mechanisms: be realistic. Don't get trapped by perfection. Revenue maximization isn't done by mathematicians. It's done by doers.

THE MELT FACTOR

When we discussed the grumblers of the stalled phase of the path to commitment, we mentioned that many executives have been disappointed by the melt factor in early revenue maximization projects. Frequently, some portion of the opportunity quantified in an earlier stage of a revenue maximization project is not captured, and the triple-scoop cone of opportunity melts to two and a half scoops of returns. Experienced revenue maximizers understand the melt factor and include it when calculating the business case and ROI. Yet some companies new to the initiative still build their business cases too aggressively.

The most common causes of the melt factor are:

- **Unanticipated business decisions.** Often, at a late stage in a project, companies choose, for instance, not to back bill a portion of the quantified leakage because of the potentially negative impact on customer retention. Other business decisions also cause individual project melt, like favoring near-term over long-term benefits. Many companies will suddenly decide to spend $5 million to capture $20 million in a series of quick-hit projects, rather than invest $4 million to seize the full $50 million opportunity with longer-term, preventive projects.

- **Capture is technically harder than anticipated.** For example, when the telecom company we discussed identified (and quantified) that it was being overcharged $1 million per year by a CLEC, immediate revenue capture demanded an intricate, time-consuming process to align the two carriers' systems.

- **Root causes are more stubborn than expected.** Many preventive capture opportunities go to the heart of how a business operates—the organically evolved day-to-day processes that dictate how a company sells, bills, or collects revenue. Reengineering processes or creating organizational change to address those long standing, obstinate root causes often takes more time than estimated.

- **Silos put up resistance.** Many projects face delays when functional cooperation is wanting, and project data, for instance, is habitually late.

Bell Canada's revenue maximization efforts provide an important lesson in the melt factor. Some of Bell Ontario's initial projects suffered considerable melt, and the project leaders had to listen to the crowing of those who doubted the project from the beginning. Still, because the leaders of the project and the business unit wholly believed in the opportunities within their companies from revenue maximization, they relentlessly pushed ahead. Equally important, the leaders kept the returns in perspective. As Mike McGrath put it to us, "At the end of the day, I didn't care if the return wasn't seven times investment. Because it still paid five times."

CONCLUSION:

REVENUE MAXIMIZATION TODAY, REVENUE MAXIMIZATION TOMORROW

We've chosen not to dwell on the dismal economic news, corporate scandals, humbling stock market performance, and iffy business outlook that surrounds us as we write this book, in the early autumn of 2002. Yes, we've mentioned the severe economic challenges in the telecom and other industries, and, yes, we've mentioned that some companies have turned to revenue maximization as a primary driver of incremental earnings growth as other growth drivers have screeched to a halt.

But we haven't dwelled on the bad news because revenue maximization is no more a strategy for a recession than it is for an expansion. Companies have made major revenue maximization gains during years of double-digit revenue growth, and they are making major gains during these bleaker days. Frankly, there is no bad time to maximize revenue.

Revenue maximization in the future. As hot as revenue maximization (or revenue assurance) has become in sectors like the telecom industry, it's not, we believe, just another fad. For the goals of the strategy—increased profitability, integrity, and growth—and the problems the strategy confronts—the inaccurate, incomplete, and untimely collection of revenue—will not go away. Nor will the temporal causes of revenue leakage: changing business landscapes, frequent mergers and acquisitions, new technologies, and rapid product development. In some industries, in fact, changes like these may accelerate further and cause even more revenue leakage in the future.

In the telecom industry, for example, the continued meltdown in profitability will almost certainly spur more consolidation, especially in sectors like wireless operators. The increasingly popular bundling of services will drive even greater complexity in pricing, provisioning, and billing. Industry-changing new technologies like 3G wireless services, IP telephony, and other data products will necessitate new billing models, new IT systems, and more opportunity for leakage. And investor and regulator scrutiny will almost certainly increase, with the equity market, the media, the SEC, and others becoming more and more unforgiving for any apparent breach of integrity.

CONCLUSION 245

Over the next five years, well-run companies with well-designed revenue maximization programs in the telecom and other industries should be able to meet these challenges. First, the principles, strategies, and tactics to conquer revenue leakage and revenue collection inaccuracies discussed in this book won't change. Only the battlefields will. Second, companies that begin now to build their expertise and experience will be able to handle future challenges faster and more efficiently. The most difficult projects now are the layups of the future. Third, technology is advancing to help. Detective, analytical, and preventive tools are becoming more powerful, more flexible, and more affordable.

So it's reasonable to assume that, within five years, many companies will have become revenue maximization enthusiasts, will have gathered all the low-hanging fruit, and will have captured many of the more challenging opportunities within their organizations. Part of us hopes that, in that time, all the advice in this book becomes commonplace because companies have institutionalized the lessons we offer and have fully maximized revenue.

Another part of us, however, doubts that this will happen, at least universally. For something will arise to distract some companies from revenue maximization and other initiatives focused on operating details—a new acquisition, maybe, or new technology, or short-term worries about survival, or a turnover in management. These distractions will prove too much for some, and they will take their eyes off the ball of timely, accurate, and complete revenue collection.

Other companies, however, with the leadership necessary to inspire and execute dynamic, comprehensive programs through the inevitable distractions, will pursue revenue maximization, and they will create real value. The companies will use this strategy as one way to distinguish themselves from the competition.

Revenue maximization now. All that being said, it's still worth mentioning the perhaps obvious point that revenue maximization is a particularly relevant strategy now. The late 1990s were a fun and exciting time for global business. Technologies seemed to create boundless markets. Customers' appetites for everything appeared insatiable. Stock prices leaped forward in 10-yard jumps. And top executives got to hammer out deals at three in the morning, helicopter into emergency board meetings, look across the table at fellow CEOs, and ask themselves, like poker players, if the other fellows were just bluffing.

For a couple of years now, that kind of fun has been harder to find. Executives now sit, staring at their stock chart, and realize that, if their stock is average, it will have to grow 60 or 70 percent to reach the level it held only two years ago. If the shock and pain and bruises are still fresh, some executives may spend their time hoping that this growth can come from P/E-multiple expansion. A few "magical thinkers" may hope that their sector will come back into favor and their stock will rebound to the boom levels of the late nineties.

Most executives, however, after the bruises begin to heal, will realize that the only way to grow their share price is, once again, to grow their company, grow their earnings, day by day, quarter by quarter. To do this, they will have to return to the nuts and bolts of the business. They will have to push for 1 and 2 percent overall revenue growth. As they have long had to do, they will have to fight for every dollar in incremental revenue, in the trenches, by hand, with operational excellence, with creativity, with grit and fearlessness and determination.

And, as our firm's global leader, Samuel DiPiazza, and PricewaterhouseCoopers' Senior Fellow Robert Eccles emphasized in their recent book, *Building Public Trust*, companies will also have to build public trust and increase their credibility with all their stakeholders.

Revenue maximization is one of the ways companies can fight by hand to deliver significant earnings growth and more assured integrity. It's not glamorous, for sure. A CEO is never going to have to call the corporate chopper to rush him or her off to Washington to close a revenue maximization project. What the strategy lacks in glamour, however, it makes up for in value. The challenges are hard, the strategies are extensive, the commitment is demanding, and the resistance is high. But the cash *available for the taking* is substantial—3, 4, or 5 percent of total revenue over one to three years.

And, as the executives we've quoted have repeated, revenue maximization, although tough, is a strategy that delivers growth without requiring a company to gain new customers or beat its competitors to the punch. It creates value from within the company. It enables a company to collect all the revenue it deserves and only the revenue it deserves from services it has already provided. In other words, it only asks executives to run their companies a little better than they are doing so today.

We are confident that leading revenue maximizers will continue to advance along the path to commitment, and more importantly, continue to create real value from revenue maximization. Even a less-than-ideal program will provide tangible and sizable benefits. (We have encouraged companies in this book to be, above all, pragmatic and to do what they can given the resources available and other corporate priorities.) And therein lies the rub. Since even modest programs create real value, there shouldn't be any excuses not to launch a program. There shouldn't be any failure.

New attitude, new commitment. We're not going to end this book by repeating the six success factors, the four core strategies, and the three-step approach. Most of these strategies and tactics are straightforward—evolutionary, not revolutionary. Yet revenue maximization is a new strategy. It demands a new intensity and a new attitude.

This new attitude is not something one can bottle and sell like ginger ale. It's sometimes even hard to describe. But anyone who has spoken to or read about a true Six Sigma zealot will recognize the new attitude. Six Sigma zealots are *offended* by a Three Sigma process, which means 93.3 percent of perfection. Most are offended by a *Four* Sigma process (99.4 percent of perfection)—not just disappointed, mind you, but offended.

Many other executives, however, sanguinely accept revenue leakage of 2 or 3 percent. This, we are certain, will change, as revenue maximization produces greater and greater value and as companies become more sophisticated in monitoring and measuring their success. Some executives will wholly adopt a new attitude. They will become personally offended by revenue leakage. They will say to themselves, "We refuse to accept *any amount of leakage* as a cost of doing business. Because our company works too hard to sell products and services. Because our company is stellar in operations. Because our company is constantly improving. Because our company will deliver profitability, integrity, and growth."

They will proclaim, Our company aggressively and relentlessly maximizes revenue.

Our company does not leak.

Index

A
Accelerated pace of product development and marketing, 50
Actions a company can take now, 139, 171, 201, 220
Asymmetry of inaccuracy, The 31

C
Caveats, The: The inexact science of ROI and the melt factor, 237
Celebrating the wins: An example from Bell Canada's Bell News, 110
Clearly defined work steps and business rules, 123
Collaborative participation of the whole revenue cycle, 190
Constant technological improvement, 163
Continuous improvement and tangible change, 193
Control mindset, The 60
Culture of extremes, A 61

D
Dabblers, The 80
Day-to-day processes, 119
Dedicated, The 84
Defensiveness, 58
Direct model, The 194
Do something, 105

E
Efficiency capture, 236
Elimination of duplication or gaps, 133
Enthusiasts, The 85
Estimated revenue leakage as percentage of total revenue in selected service-sector industries, 22
Exceptions complex, The 60
Executive support and leadership, 178

F
Fight for quantifiable monitoring mechanisms, 219
Finance matrix model, The 196
Five key features of an automated tool strategy, The 148
Five key features of day-to-day processes, The 122
Formal diagnostics, 225
Formal revenue maximization function, A 187
Four core strategies of revenue maximization, The 9
Frequency mergers and acquisitions, 47

G
Guiding principles for quantifiable monitoring mechanisms, 217

H
Help is available, 115
How do you do it?, 6

I
Identify, quantify, capture approach, 224
Identify, quantify, capture, 223
Immediate capture, 231
In praise of self-reliance, 114
Individual management and accountability, 130
Industry paths follow industry dynamics, 91
Inexact science of ROI, The 237
Integrate revenue maximization processes into all change, 136
Investments are low and so is the risk, The 27

K
Key automated tools, 145
Key features of a revenue responsible organization, 178
Key features of an automated tools strategy, 149
Keys to success: Managing a Revenue Maximazation Initiative, 93

M
Manage success, 108
Measurability of results, 132
Measured participation of all levels of management, 182
Melt factor, The 239
Moving up the path to commitment, 88

O
Operations matrix model, The 197
Opportunity capture, 235

P
Path to commitment, The 76, 77
People: We're only human, 64
Periodically calculate and update metrics, 217
Potential core members of formal revenue maximization function, 189
Preventive capture, 233
Processes, 67
Proposition #1: Growth, 19
Proposition #2: Profitability, 25
Proposition #3: Integrity, 29
Proximate causes: Technology, people, and processes, 61

Q
Quantifiable monitoring mechanisms, 205
Quantifiable monitoring mechanisms bond and embed all strategies, 206
Quantifiable returns, 29

R
Rapid adoption of new technologies, 49
Rapidly changing competitive landscapes and business models, 51
Resistant, The 77
Resources, 184
Returns are High, The 26
Revenue maximization today, revenue maximization tomorrow, 243
Revenue responsible organization, The 175

S
Sample leaks in two industries, 39
Sample revenue maximization dashboard, 158
Sample telecom industry diagnostic question, 227
Sample tier 1 revenue maximization metrics, 208

INDEX

Sample tiered metrics, 216
See the forest and the trees, 100
Silo mentality, The 54
Simplify, integrate, tier, 210
Six facts about revenue leakage, 37
Six key features of a revenue responsible organization, The 177
Six keys to success, 96
Some overlapping revenue maximization terms, 7
Speak in dollars and cents, 101
Speciation point, The 75
Stalled, The 82
Step #1: Identify, 225
Step #2: Quantify, 228
Strategic overview, 8
Susceptibilities: The cultural causes, 53

T
Technology, 62
Telecom industry focuses on leakage, The 73
Temporal causes: Change causes leaks, 46
Three causes of revenue leakage, 46
Three causes of revenue leaks, 45
Three objections, 4
Three revenue maximization organizational models, 195
Tier, 214
Tools as a living part of company operations, 165
Two questions, 198

U
Use of analytical tools, 156
Use of detective tools, 149
Use of preventive tools, 158

V
Value propositions, The 3
Value propositions: Growth, profitability and integrity, The 17
Value propositions of revenue maximization, 19
Very short history of revenue maximization, A 72

W
What a company can, can't, and should do itself, 113
What companies are doing now, 71
What's new about revenue maximization?, 5
What's the best organizational structure?, 193
Where's the proof?, 24
Why monitoring mechanisms are important, 208
Why revenue maximization?, 01